POST-EUROPE

Yuk Hui

T0244551

URBANOMIC

sequence

For Miyako

In its common concept, autobiographical anamnesis presupposes identification. And precisely not identity. No, an identity is never given, received, or attained; only the interminable and indefinitely phantasmatic process of identification endures.

—Jacques Derrida, *Monolingualism of the Other*

CONTENTS

PREFACE

This work takes up threads from *The Question Concerning Technology in China*[1] concerning the question of homecoming or, more precisely, the problem of homelessness [*Heimatlosigkeit*] as a consequence of modernisation and planetarisation. Seven years after the publication of that book, the world has changed in ways that have rendered it barely recognisable. Three years of pandemic only served to accelerate geopolitical shifts which seem to be speeding the planet into turmoil, whether in the shape of imminent wars or climate collapse. We live more than ever in a state of becoming-homeless, while paradoxically this homelessness also produces a desire to be at home, as is evident in recent conservative and neoreactionary movements. During the summer of 2016, our late lamented young friend Damian Veal, while copyediting *The Question Concerning Technology in China*, questioned whether my attempt to reconstruct a Chinese thinking of technology was not following exactly the same path as Heidegger, and courting the same ideological fallacy to which he fell prey. As I summarised in the book, partly as a response to Damian's concerns, there is a difficulty here concerning the dilemma of homecoming.

Seven years later, this dilemma seems to me to be increasingly challenging and disturbing in view of the increase in territorial conflicts and racialised politics. How can philosophy today respond to this call for a homecoming that has been described as constituting its very possibility (Novalis's claim that philosophy is driven by homesickness), but which has also called it into question since the twentieth century? In trying to answer this question about homecoming I was forced to confront myself, my own experience as a constant wanderer and immigrant: What does *Heimat* mean for an immigrant

1. Y. Hui, *The Question Concerning Technology in China: An Essay in Cosmotechnics* (Falmouth: Urbanomic, 2016).

like me, continually obliged to adapt to new environments and to learn new languages? I was also forced to formulate certain things I had had in mind, but had not been able to properly articulate, all those years ago. Hence this book can also be read as an autobiography, albeit one in which the 'I' is absent, or more precisely where the 'I' is absorbed by different figures at different points.

The title *Post-Europe* is a reference to the proposal of the phenomenologist Jan Patočka, who observed that, after the Second World War, Europe ceased to be a central power. This epochal event, according to Patočka, also acted as a moment of *epochē* in the phenomenological sense: the old concept of Europe was suspended and a new Europe could emerge from this suspension. Post-Europe could mean many things: the United States, thought to be the new Europe in the nineteenth century, a Europe that is no longer, or a new world situation after the European Enlightenment. Like Heidegger, Patočka looked for the source of a new Europe in ancient Greece, and especially in Plato's doctrine of the soul—without however acknowledging the fact that Europe has been always defined in opposition to Asia. When we speak about post-Europe today, do we mean a world in which Asia will dominate, as certain political propaganda from the East provokes us to imagine? Philosophy becomes worthless when it becomes an echo of political propaganda, but alas, how many philosophers can refuse even the slightest temptation to become a state thinker?

What else could European philosophy become, after the constant call for de-Europeanisation and repeated proposals for a post-Europe over past decades? How might philosophy respond to the Other of Europe in the planetary condition? And how might the Other respond to the European legacy, beyond trivial criticisms of Eurocentrism? It is with these questions in mind that this 'autobiography' unfolds by way of an *incompatibility* incarnated both in bodily experience and in the thinking process. Through this tension, what unfolds here is also a process of *individuation*, in Gilbert Simondon's sense. In this way, I seek to explore how the concept of individuation can be taken beyond the domains in which Simondon, and later Bernard Stiegler, put it to work. Individuation is conditioned by tensions or incompatibilities between elements within a system. Perhaps it is precisely in a system where two kinds of thinking cannot be immediately reconciled that we might rephrase Heidegger's question 'What is called thinking?', asking instead 'What is called the individuation of thinking?'

The two main chapters in this book are based on two lectures that I gave at Taipei National University of the Arts in December 2022 upon the kind invitation of the president of the university, Professor Chen Kai-Huang. Professor Chen had invited Bernard Stiegler and myself to Taipei previously, in Autumn 2019, for a series of master-classes, where we also discussed the possibility of establishing a laboratory in the university's new building dedicated to technology and art, which was still under construction. This was also the last time I saw Bernard, who is one of the two principal figures engaged with in the first chapter. The second chapter is a response to post-colonial discourses on Asia and the question of the future of Asian thought, and explains what I mean by 'individuation of thinking' through the figures of Mou Zongsan and Kitaro Nishida, two of the most original thinkers to have emerged from Asia in the twentieth century.

The broader idea for this project came from my long-term interest in the 'Overcoming Modernity' project that the Kyoto School philosophers initiated a century ago. (A famous symposium organized by the magazine *Bungakukai* bearing the same title took place in July 1942.) We know that history repeats itself, and that in its repetition it always appears as a form of *déjà vu*. In 1941 and 1942, during the outbreak of the Second World War, four philosophers and historians from the Kyoto School participated in three symposiums organised by the literature magazine *Chūō Kōron* (中央公論, *Central Review*). In the first of these symposiums, entitled 'The Standpoint of World History and Japan', Asia was placed in opposition to Europe and, in view of the decline of the Occident, it was proposed that Asia, or more precisely Japan, would have to take up the duty of forging world history. Today, almost a century later, we see this proposal being repeated with different rhetoric.

As a response to this repetition, *Post-Europe* opens with a prelude entitled 'The Standpoint of *Heimatlosigkeit*' and ends with a coda on 'The Good Post-Europeans'.

Lastly, I would like to add that this book is a meditation on the tongue, a technical organ which is no less important than the hands. The book starts with the question of taste and closes with that of language, the two most important functions of the tongue.

During the spring of 2023, thanks to the invitation of the Tokyo College, I had the opportunity to spend two months at the University of Tokyo. I was welcomed by Professor Tsuyoshi Ishii, Professor Ching-Yuen Cheung, and other colleagues. Professor Takahiro Nakajima, the director of the Institute of Advanced Studies on Asia at Todai, was kind enough to invite me to use his library on the Hongō campus, where I was able to read many original texts on overcoming modernity and the Kyoto School that I hadn't been able to access before. This time in Japan was crucial for the completion of the book. I would like to take this opportunity to thank colleagues who have been engaging with my thinking throughout this journey, including Kohei Ise, Daisuke Harashima, Hidetaka Ishida, Masaki Fujihata, Agnes Lin, Johnson Chang, Hugo Esquinca, Milan Stürmer, Pieter Lemmens, and especially Hiroki Azuma with whom I have had many conversations on this topic since we first met in 2016, which have always been amicable and productive. I want to thank Sequence Press and Urbanomic for their joint force in publishing this book, especially Maya B. Kronic's meticulous editorial and critical comments.

Yuk Hui
Autumn 2023
Rotterdam and Taipei

PRELUDE

The STANDPOINT of *HEIMATLOSIGKEIT*

Homelessness is coming to be the destiny of the world.

—Martin Heidegger[1]

Can we continue to regard, as Husserl does, the Chinese, Indians and Persians as 'anthropological types of humanity', and these societies of the past as devoid of problematicity, as Patočka suggests, or as mere private economies, as Hannah Arendt asserts? In my view, it is urgently necessary at the start of the twenty-first cetury for philosophers to develop the historical sense that Nietzsche said they so sorely lack, and to recognise that these discourses on Europe are no more than an ideological construct and the result of a conception of the world that stems from colonialism, with which, unfortunately, the name Europe remains closely linked.

—Françoise Dastur[2]

§1. PLANETARISATION and *HEIMATLOSIGKEIT*

In the eighteenth century, philosophy was described by Novalis as a kind of suffering, a homesickness and a longing to be at home: 'Philosophy is actually homesickness—*the desire to be everywhere at home* [*Die Philosophie sei eigentlich Heimweh—Trieb, überall zu Hause zu sein*]'.[3] The *Heim-* here is not only home, but more significantly invokes a *homeland* [*Heimat*]. This longing for *Heimat* became an omnipresent phenomenon during the process of colonisation and modernisation. But during the same period, home become a mere

1. M. Heidegger, 'Letter on Humanism', in *Pathmarks*, ed. W. McNeill, tr. F.A. Capuzzi (Cambridge: Cambridge University Press, 1998), 258.
2. F. Dastur, 'L'Europe et ses philosophes: Nietzsche, Husserl, Heidegger, Patocka', *Revue Philosophique de Louvain* 104:1 (2006): 8.
3. Novalis, *Notes for a Romantic Encyclopedia: Das Allgemeine Brouillon*, ed., tr. D.W. Wood (New York: SUNY Press, 2007), 155.

geographical location upon one particular celestial body (among countless others), and the importance of a geographical location began to be evaluated in terms of its abundance of natural resources and its economic potential. One may, like Heidegger, remember the pathway of the *Heimat* in summer, the old linden trees gazing over the garden wall; a pathway that shines bright between growing crops and waking meadows.[4] But today the small village is full of tourists who want to visit the *Heimat* of a famous philosopher, and new infrastructure is being built to accommodate the demands of these visitors from all over the world. Alas, the *Heimat* ceases to be what it once was.

Economic and technological development has continued to alter the landscape of these small villages, and in even more radical ways with advances in the automatisation of agriculture. Today many rural areas are using drones and robots to fully automate the processes of sowing, ploughing, harvesting, packing, transportation, etc. The farmers no longer resemble the old lady that Heidegger once imagined when seeing Van Gogh's painting of the 'peasant's shoes'. Today's farmers are young, dress in smart suits, and control all operations with their iPads. The village remains, as do the linden trees and meadows, but the surrounding area is gentrified with expensive cafés and hotels, and the route of Heidegger's pathway is intersected by the vectors of drones and robots. This lends an even more hysterical tone to the philosopher's exclamation when we read it today:

> Man's attempts to bring order to the world by his plans will remain futile as long as he is not ordered to the call of the pathway. The danger looms that men today cannot hear its language. The only thing they hear is the noise of the media, which they almost take for the voice of God. So man becomes

---

4. M. Heidegger, 'The Pathway', tr. T.F. O'Meara and T. Sheehan, in
    T. Sheehan (ed.), *Heidegger: The Man and the Thinker* (Chicago: Precedent,
    1981), 69.

disoriented and loses his way. To the disoriented, the simple seems monotonous. The monotonous brings weariness, and the weary and bored find only what is uniform. The simple has fled. Its quiet power is exhausted.[5]

The longing for *Heimat* is a consequence of a sense of being away from home—the nearest and the remotest to us, as Heidegger says, it is so close and so far that we fail to see it.[6] One might well continually travel from continent to continent. However, there seems to be only one home, to which one would finally return when one feels tired and no longer wants to move. Over past centuries, the conception of the home as the place of natality has been altered owing to the increasing prevalence of immigrants and refugees. From the standpoint of *Heimat*, immigration is an uprooting event in which the plant has to search for a new soil in which to implant itself. However, even if the new soil provides the appropriate nutrients, the immigrant's memory of *Heimat* always reminds one of a past that is no longer and will never be again. And, being foreign, they will also have changed the existing soil by bringing about a new ecological configuration. The moderns begin to sense their homelessness upon the earth, as described by Georg Trakl in his poem 'Springtime of the Soul':

> Something strange is the soul on the earth. Ghostly
>   the twilight
> Bluing over the mishewn forest, and a dark bell
> Long tolls in the village; they lead him to rest.[7]

5. Ibid., 70.
6. J. Young, 'Heidegger's Heimat', *International Journal of Philosophical Studies* 19:2 (2011): 285.
7. Cited in M. Heidegger, 'Language in the Poem: A Discussion on George Trakl's Poetic Art', in *On the Way to Language*, tr. P.D. Hertz (New York: Harper & Row, 1971), 198.

This feeling of *Heimatlosigkeit* haunted thinkers of the twentieth century, for whom the most important philosophical task became that
of shedding light upon a *Heimat* to come. The soul is a stranger on
the earth, where any place is rendered *unheimisch* (*unhomely*). For
Heidegger, homecoming is an orientation [*Erörterung*] which defines
a locality as a root without which nothing can grow. However, when
homelessness becomes the destiny of the world, the soul is comparable to a green houseplant, in the sense that it could be grown and
taken anywhere on the planet. The homogenisation of the planet
through techno-economic activities has created a synchronicity of
social phenomena. Rituals and heritage sites become fodder for
tourists, with mobile phone cameras replacing the senses of the eyes
and the body. The soul's relation to the world is mediated through
digital apparatuses and platforms.

However, memory is not simply a cognitive entity in the mind.
The interiority of the body also struggles to fully adapt to the new
environment. Food can then become the strongest reminder of a
past, like the madeleine crumbs dipped in lime blossom tea that
Proust described in his *In Search of Lost Time*. This experience is
even more common when one lives abroad. We might not be able
to identify such an experience in the writings of Heidegger, since
the philosopher never travelled outside of Europe, but we can find
it described by his foreign students. Keiji Nishitani, one of the rep-
resentatives of the Kyoto School, spent two years in Freiburg with
Heidegger between 1937 and 1939. On a September day in 1938,
together with two other Japanese students, Nishitani was invited
to dinner by Fumi Takahashi, the niece of Kitaro Nishida, who
had just arrived in Freiburg in April 1938 to study with Heidegger.[8]
Takahashi cooked a Japanese meal with ingredients she had brought
from Japan. Nishitani, who at the time had been living on a German
diet for more than a year,[9] upon tasting the bowl of white rice, felt
something extraordinary, as James Heisig remarked:

8. See M. Yusa, *Zen & Philosophy: An Intellectual Biography of Nishida Kitarō*
   (Honolulu: University of Hawai'i Press, 2002), 243.

Eating his first bowl of rice after a steady diet of Western food, [Nishitani] was overwhelmed by an 'absolute taste' that went beyond the mere quality of the food.[10]

Imagine if Heidegger had taught in Japan: would he have been able to put *Schwäbische Küche* out of his mind and body while eating sashimi and sushi? Probably not. In the case of Nishitani, the *Heimweh* arrived when *shirogohan* instead of *Kornbrot* stimulated the taste buds, but the sensation also went beyond the taste buds and affected the whole body.[11] *Heimat* is not to do with what one learns of one's nation in a history lesson, but rather is something inscribed in the body as one of its most intimate and inexplicable parts. This experience of being *Unheimlich* (*uncanny*)[12] only reinforces the longing for *Heimat*. As Nishitani concludes, in his memoir of this meal:

This same experience also made me think about what is called 'homeland,' which is fundamentally that of the inseparable

9. Nishitani wrote about this experience in a short article published in a magazine thirty-three years after this meal. The article bears the title, 'The Experience of Eating Rice' (飯を喰つた經驗), it was later republished in the collected work of Nishitani, see K. Nishitani, '飯を喰つた經驗', in *NKC* 20 (西谷啓治著作集) (Tokyo: Shobunsha, 1990), 196–202.

10. J. Heisig, *Philosophers of Nothingness: An Essay on the Kyoto School* (Honolulu: University of Hawai'i Press, 2001); see also Nishitani, 'The Experience of Eating Rice', 197: '強ひて言へば絶對的な旨さである。'.

11. Nishitani, 'The Experience of Eating Rice', 197: '舌の上では なく全身で感ずる旨さである。'

12. In his lecture course on Hölderlin's Hymn 'The Ister', Heidegger reintroduces the term *unheimisch*, which is now much less used than *unheimlich* in German. Heidegger wants to reassociate the meaning of *unheimisch* (unhomely, or not being at home) with *unheimlich* (uncanny, strangeness), see M. Heidegger, *Hölderlin's Hymn 'The Ister'* (Indianapolis: Indiana University Press, 1996); *Hölderlins Hymne »Der Ister« GA 53* (Frankfurt am Main: Vittorio Klostermann, 1993).

relation between the soil and the human being, in particular the human being as a body. It is 'the nonduality of soil and body' of which Buddhism speaks. In my case, homeland is the 'Land of Vigorous Rice Plants': a soil fit for rice and a people that has found the mainstay of its livelihood in rice cultivation. From generation to generation, my ancestors have had rice as their staple food. The special ingredients of the land called Japan are transferred to the special ingredients of the rice called 'Japanese rice', and through eating rice, they are transferred to the 'blood' of our ancestors, and that blood flows through my body. Perhaps from long ago, the vital connection between the countless people who were my ancestors, the rice, and the land has always been the background of my life and is actually contained in it. This experience made me remember something that I had usually forgotten.[13]

The bowl of white rice is not just food that satisfies biological need, negating the sense of hunger; it is also a mediation between body and *Heimat*. Taste is associated with the Fatherland via the tongue. It is no surprise, then, that after returning to Japan, Nishitani actively participated in the movement of 'overcoming modernity', which

---

13. 同じ經驗はまた、私に「國土」といふものを考へさせた。國土の觀念は基本的には、土地と人間、特に身體としての人間の不可分な聯關を意味してゐる。佛教で「身土不二」といはれたことである。私の場合には、「瑞穗の國」といはれたやうな、稻に適した土地、そこで稻作りを主な生計にして來た民族である。私の先祖も代々、米を主食にしてゐたてあらう。日本といふ土地の特殊な成分が、「日本米」といふ米の特殊な成分にうつり、米食を通して先祖代々の「血」にうつり、その血が私の身體のうちにも流れてゐる。いつの昔からか、私の祖先であつた數知れぬ人々と米と國土との生命的な聯關が、私のいのちの背景となり、現に私のいのちに含まれてゐる。かの經驗は普段忘れてゐたその事實を、私に想ひ起させたのである。Nishitani, 'The Experience of Eating Rice', 202. Also cited in J. Heisig, *Philosophers of Nothingness: An Essay on the Kyoto School* (Honolulu: University of Hawai'i Press, 2001), 214, I have expanded Heisig's citation.

gathered historians, music critics, philosophers, and literary scholars to reflect upon how to overcome the domination and the decadence of Europe. To them, European modernity presented itself as a fragmenting force, its separation of culture into religion, science, and politics (or more precisely democracy) destroying the unified world view which, in Japanese and Chinese culture, held together heaven, earth, and the human.[14] However, even as this European nihilism continued to spread across the entire globe, Europe itself was declining. The Europeanisation of the East then also threatened to introduce the East into the same decadence as the West. In his book *Self-Overcoming Nihilism* (a collection of lectures on nihilism delivered in 1949), commenting on Karl Löwith's essay 'European Nihilism', Nishitani asked what European nihilism meant to Japan:

> European nihilism thus brought a radical change in our relationship to Europe and to ourselves. It now forces our actual historical existence, our 'being ourselves among others', to take a radically new direction. It no longer allows us simply to rush into westernization while forgetting ourselves.[15]

The twentieth century was a century of orienting [*erörteren*] *Heimat* within the planetarisation of European modernity. Although he made it possible for Nishitani and Tanabe to go and study abroad in Germany, Kitaro Nishida himself didn't have the chance to do so when he was young. Yet in his writing one can also find this search for *Heimat*—which for him bears the name of East Asia, or *tōyō*. This longing for *Heimat* continues to intensify because modernisation implies the destruction of the old and the creation of something

---

14. See Nishitani's talk 'My View on "Overcoming Modernity"' (「近代の超克」私論) in Tetsutarō Kawakami and Yoshimi Takeuchi (eds.), *Overcoming Modernity* (近代の超克) (Tokyo: Fuzambo, 1979), 18–37.

15. K. Nishitani, *The Self-Overcoming of Nihilism*, tr. G. Parkes with S. Aihara (New York: SUNY Press, 1990), 179.

that is global. The destruction of villages and forests for the sake of building new infrastructure, the renovation of urban spaces in order to accommodate tourism and foster real estate development, the increasing immigrant and refugee population—all of these created a feeling of being *unheimisch*. And then after Europeanisation there came Americanisation or Americanism, of which Heidegger and his Japanese students were already very conscious, and which they regarded as the continuation of Europeanisation through a planned planetarisation.[16] In 'What are Poets For?', an essay dedicated to Rilke, Heidegger cited the poet's letter to Witold Hulewicz in 1925 on the Americanisation of Europe:

> For our grandparents a 'house,' a 'well,' a familiar steeple, even their own clothes, their cloak *still* meant infinitely more, were infinitely more intimate—almost everything a vessel in which they found something human already there, and added to its human store. Now there are intruding, from America, empty, indifferent things, sham things, *dummies of*

---

16. M. Heidegger, 'The Age of the World Picture', in *The Question Concerning Technology and Other Essays*, tr. W. Lovitt (New York: Harper and Row, 1977), 153. '"Americanism" is itself something European. It is an as-yet uncomprehended variety of the gigantic, and the gigantic itself is still inchoate, still not yet capable of being understood as the product of the full and complete metaphysical essence of modernity. The American interpretation of Americanism by means of pragmatism still remains outside the metaphysical realm.' In this sense, Americanism is no different from Sovietism, as announced by Heidegger in *Introduction to Metaphysics* as follows: 'This Europe, in its ruinous blindness forever on the point of cutting its own throat, lies today in a great pincers, squeezed between Russia on one side and America on the other. From a metaphysical point of view, Russia and America are the same; the same dreary technological frenzy, the same unrestricted organization of the average man.' M. Heidegger, *An Introduction to Metaphysics*, tr. R. Mannheim (Garden City, NJ: Anchor, 1961), 38–39.

life [*Lebensattrappe*].... A house, as the Americans understand it, an American apple or a winestock from over there, have *nothing* in common with the house, the fruit, the grape into which the hope and thoughtfulness of our forefathers had entered.... Things living, experienced, and communing are going under and cannot be replaced. We are perhaps the last ones who will have known such things.[17]

The ultimate problem for Heidegger was inhuman technology.[18] Modern technology is the end product of European nihilism, which began with the forgetting of the question of Being and the effort to master [*beherrschen*] beings. The interposition of technology into the world has produced a generalised homelessness, and has blocked the path toward the questioning of Being. *Heimatlosigkeit* is tantamount to the *Heillosigkeit* (unholiness or hopelessness) of the *Abendland*, the evening land, in the dawn of Americanism and its imperial force, supported by its planetary technologies. Again in 'What are Poets For?', we read Heidegger's clearest lament on this matter:

The essence of technology comes to the light of day only slowly. This day is the world's night, rearranged into merely technological day. This day is the shortest day. It threatens a single endless winter. Not only does protection now withhold itself from man, but the integralness of the whole of what is remains now in darkness. The wholesome and sound withdraws. The world becomes without healing, unholy. Not only does the holy,

17. Rainer Maria Rilke to Witold Hulewicz, 13 November 1925, *Briefe in Zwei Bänden* (Wiesbaden: Insel Verlag, 2 vols., 1950), vol. 2, 376–77; quoted in M. Heidegger, *Poetry, Language, Thought* (New York: Harper and Row, 1971), 110–11.

18. G. Günther, 'Heidegger und die Weltgeschichte des Nichts', in *Nachdenken über Heidegger: eine Bestandsaufnahme*, ed. U. Guzzoni (Hildesheim: Gerstenberg, 1980), 83.

as the track to the godhead, thereby remain concealed; even the track to the holy, the hale and whole, seems to be effaced.[19]

In the age of technology, Being withdraws from the world; what is left is a world of beings decomposed into atoms and feedback loops. This uprooting [*Entwurzelung*], for Heidegger, is no longer a phenomenon of the West, it has gone beyond Europe through its planetary technology. One might recall here Tolstoy's criticism voiced in 1910, during his last years, when the writer said that mediaeval theology or the Roman moral inheritance only intoxicated a limited amount of people, but today's electricity, trains, and telegraph have intoxicated the whole world.[20]

These technologies are carriers of Western thinking, Western models of individuation, modes of production, and a Western libidinal economy. Economy first of all consists in exchanges of technics and technicity that short-circuit the process of production: for example, the tool we buy in the market is produced via a complex technical system, but we can simply use it without having to learn how to make it ourselves. But at the same time, the economic system demands technology as its medium of exchange, ranging from cargo transportation to high-speed trading. In his lecture 'What is Called Thinking?' Heidegger mocks *logistics* as the most recent and fruitful realisation of 'logic', which in many Anglo-Saxon countries, he says, is considered the 'only possible form of strict philosophy'.[21]

In the twenty-first century, we can easily sense that this process of destruction and recreation is only accelerating rather than slowing down. The longing for *Heimat* will only be intensified

---

19. Heidegger, 'What are Poets For?', 115.

20. See K. Löwith, 'Der europäische Nihilismus. Betrachtungen zur Vorgeschichte des europäischen Krieges', in *Weltgeschichte und Heilsgeschehen: Zur Kritik der Geschichtsphilosophie* (Stuttgart: J.B. Metzlersche, 1983), 497.

21. M. Heidegger, *What is Called Thinking?*, tr. F.D. Wiieck and J.G. Gray (New York: Harper & Row, 1968), 21.

instead of being diminished; the dilemma of homecoming can only become more pathological. In fact, two opposed movements are taking place at the same time: planetarisation and homecoming. Capital and techno-science, with their assumed universality, have a tendency toward escalation and self-propagation, while the specificity of territory and customs have a tendency to resist what is foreign.

Homecoming is being challenged in very concrete ways today. When we look into the housing problem in Europe in 2023, the amount of people who cannot afford to rent a proper apartment for their family has sharply increased. The increase in property prices over the past decade is alarming. This may continue until a certain moment when the bubble bursts, and then those who are paying mortgages will be in unmanageable debt. Global real estate speculation and the neoliberal economy have created a situation of *Heimatlosigkeit* which challenges both *ethos* and *ethics*. This real estate speculation will continue to drain the creativity and potential of individuals.

2023–2024 have been marked by a feeling that the world has begun to fall apart. On the one hand there is the Russia-Ukraine War—a constant reminder of the insecurity of Europe and the cause of a global logistical catastrophe; at the moment of writing, the Israel-Hamas War appears to be far more brutal and inhuman, and displays clear indications that another world war could erupt at any time. On the other hand, rapid technological acceleration, emblematised by ChatGPT, invokes the sentiment that the human will be rendered obsolete by machines very soon. Deracination is accelerated by technology because machines are capable of learning in order to outdo human competitors. Well beyond the triumph of AlphaGo, which was limited to the Go game, AI has now penetrated into almost all domains of everyday activity and is disrupting them, turning them upside down. This technological, ecological, and economic progress clearly promises us some kind of apocalypse.

This ruin caused by techno-economic planetarisation calls for a homecoming, a return to the *ethos*. The world is once again being seen from the standpoint of *Heimat*, but not from a planetary perspective nor that of world history. Frustration and discontent at no longer being at home express themselves as wars against outsiders, with immigrants and refugees the first targets of discrimination and hatred. Reactionaries and neoreactionaries want to return home—to a home that was once 'great', and which one must make great once again. According to some, especially those who believe in the 'deep state', the death of the community, described in terms of a 'Great Replacement', also means the end of the individual, since by that point Europe would be 'blackwashed'.[22]

The process of planetarisation has produced a global disorientation. Does this mean that we need to reconstruct the concept of *Heimat*? Does this call for another *Blut und Boden*? Can the return to *Heimat* help us to escape this process of increasing alienation? We already know the answer. For the twentieth century was a century of searching for *Heimat*. The philosophical movement associated with it was reactionary and dangerous. Everyone certainly needs a 'home' or a locality where they feel safe and at ease. But this home is not necessarily the same as the search for *Heimat*, or fatherland, found in literature beginning in the eighteenth century and which persists in the online reactionary tracts of today.

§2. The AFFIRMATION of *HEIMATLOSIGKEIT*

One might feel at ease being at home. As everyone knows, mother tongue and family networks may not make life less onerous, but they do make access to certain things much easier. A Japanese colleague living in London once told me that he couldn't eat British vegetables, and that his wife had to buy vegetables freshly delivered from Japan at the Japan Centre in Leicester Square. But he still

---

22. For example, in the work of the conspiracy theorist and white nationalist Renaud Camus.

didn't feel at home, because when he went to meetings at the university, even though he worked in a Japanese Studies department, the standpoint was always British or pan-European. In the end he decided to go back to Japan, where he felt at home. Another friend's mother loved the old Bahnhof in Stuttgart; after her death, as a native German, he managed to acquire a stone from the Bahnhof and used it as a gravestone for her. For an immigrant living in Germany, such a gesture would be near impossible because the amount of bureaucracy one would need to go through would be too exhausting.

This is not something that Immanuel Kant could have imagined, because the great philosopher of cosmopolitanism never left Königsberg (now Kaliningrad in Russia). According to Kant, world citizenship grants a 'right of resort' or right to hospitality. He argued that the earth is shared by everyone, and that one should have the right to visit other countries and be welcomed as a guest. And he was quite right: the earth shouldn't be regarded as someone's private property, and one ought to have the right to wander on this planet without being harmed or arrested. Even if one is refused from entering the country, it should not be done with hostility.

However, the concept of world citizenship is still built upon an opposition between home and non-home, internal and external. Today, the right of visitation (to non-home, external nations) is contested by the ownership of all kinds of resources including natural and human resources, and the foreigner's activities are limited to sightseeing and shopping. The concepts of the border and the visa, inventions in the name of national security, are grounded upon the concept of private property and the household. In many Western modern states, a good citizen is a good taxpayer; naturalisation is evaluated according to the amount of tax and pension one has paid. Today we have tourists who are not entitled to work in foreign countries, but who have the right to travel—provided that their passport, the symbol of the status of their *Heimat*, is strong enough. The Japanese, for instance, have the right to visit more than one hundred and ninety countries without a visa, while Afghans in 2023 could go to no more than thirty countries.

In 'Christianity or Europe' (1799), Novalis reproached the uni-formity of reason he sensed in the work of Enlightenment thinkers, and romanticised the 'beautiful and splendid times' of the Middle Ages, when love and faith effectively suppressed individualism and violence.[23] But what Novalis regarded as a cosmopolitanism has become paradoxically anti-cosmopolitan because, once again, it has turned to a longing or nostalgia for a *Heimat* which is no longer. What might be the response of philosophy in the twen-ty-first century when confronting the techno-economic force that seems to have put an end to so many beliefs of the past? Can we only envision the annihilation of technology as an antidote to the annihilation of nature? If *Heimat* was the condition of world cit-izenship, what happened to the world citizen when we entered into an epoch of *Heimatlosigkeit*? Heidegger does far more than just denounce technology: consider his reference to the mysteri-ous verse of Hölderlin's *Patmos*, 'But where the danger is, grows the saving power also.' This is comparable to what Hegel called the cunning of reason: the danger is a constant reminder of a dif-ferent path which sheds light upon the question of Being. Thus, if modern technology means the end or completion of Western phi-losophy and metaphysics, then something has to arise from such an end, something that exceeds technological enframing [*Gestell*].

Heidegger answered these questions with 'the other beginning', and Derrida responded with 'the other heading'.[24] Heidegger was still haunted by *Heimat*, but such a *Heimat* in the end was no longer the black forest but Greece, a Greece seen as both beginning and end. The return to Greece is a recursive movement; however, the comple-tion of the loop took more than two and a half thousand years. Are we now entering into another loop, or are we heading elsewhere?

23. See P. Kleingeld, 'Romantic Cosmopolitanism: Novalis's "Christianity or Europe"', *Journal of the History of Philosophy* 46:2 (2008): 269–84.
24. J. Derrida, *The Other Heading Reflections on Today's Europe*, tr. P.-A. Brault and M.B. Naas (Indianapolis: Indiana University Press, 1992).

Didn't Heidegger then play the role of Hyperion, and in this sense, isn't Heidegger united with Hölderlin?

Heimatlosigkeit will continue to be a characteristic of twenty-first-century planetarisation unless a conservative revolution takes place everywhere in the world and all of a sudden the world order is changed, as Fichte imagined in *The Closed Commercial State* (1800), in which he proposed that each state should close off its commercial activities from other states. Today Fichte could be regarded as a thinker of anti-globalisation; his proposal could be read in today's vocabulary as 'decoupling'. Since 2019, the United States and China have entered into a trade war; during the pandemic, China, a communist regime, accused the US, a capitalist regime, of being anti-globalisation and damaging the free market. This would have been unimaginable during the 1990s, when the US was the strongest promoter of globalisation and when free market ideology announced the 'end of history'. One could certainly read this dialectically, and propose the end of the end of history as a negation of negation; however, this does not really enlighten us much further than affording the satisfactions of playing a dialectical game.

Can we take *Heimatlosigkeit* further as a *default*, then? Or as a *fate*, even? If we don't look at the world from the standpoint of home, can we look at it from the perspective of *Heimatlosigkeit*? Namely, could we try to engage with this world from the perspective of ruins—the ruins that are produced by economic and technological globalisation? World history, we could then say, is a history of liberation from *Heimat*, which was initially physically bounded, and later came to be defined culturally. But what would it mean to think from the standpoint of *Heimatlosigkeit*?

In this sense, maybe Jean-François Lyotard has already given us some hints with his thesis on the postmodern. The postmodern condition is a technological condition, in the sense that technological development has sublated the modernity that produced it. If the modern began with a sense of certainty and security, as in Descartes's meditations, where such certainty is the only possible beginning of knowledge and its guarantee, the postmodern condition is one under which knowledge no longer emanates from the human subject. Instead, technologies—robotics, artificial intelligence, databases, synthetic biology, etc.—exceed human-centred knowledge production and subvert the relation between the subject and its knowledge. Under the postmodern condition, one no longer finds oneself at home. Instead, one finds oneself in an insecure and uncertain world which is at the same time open and fearful. The postmodern is today largely understood as an aesthetics or a genre of literature or cinema, but for Lyotard it was far more than that. The postmodern condition gestures towards the questioning of the significance of not being at home, of being *unheimisch* and *unheimlich*.

The standpoint is shifted, the world is turned upside down. When Husserl wrote his polemical essay 'The Original Ark, the Earth, Does Not Move',[25] he was also thinking of the earth as a home, but not as a celestial body, as Copernicus had treated it. Husserl wasn't wrong, and neither was Copernicus, but whether the phenomenological method is superior to the mathematical method is another issue. We are told by Nietzsche that 'since Copernicus, man has been rolling from the centre toward X',[26] faster and faster into nothingness; and yet after Copernicus, the philosophy of the subjective prevailed, as Descartes's meditations restored the human being to its status as the origin of all certainty. Later, Husserl's *Cartesian*

25. E. Husserl, 'Foundational Investigations of the Phenomenological Origin of the Spatiality of Nature: The Originary Ark, the Earth, Does Not Move', in M. Merleau-Ponty, *Husserl at the Limits of Phenomenology Including Texts by Edmund Husserl*, tr. L. Lawlor and B. Bergo (Evanston, IL: Northwestern University Press, 2001), 117–31.

26. 'The nihilistic consequences of contemporary natural science (together with its attempts to escape into some beyond). The industry of its pursuit eventually leads to self-disintegration, opposition, an antiscientific mentality. Since Copernicus man has been rolling from the center toward X.' F. Nietzsche, *The Will to Power*, tr. W. Kaufmann and R.J. Hollingdale (New York: Vintage, 1968), 8.

Meditations attempted to give the most indubitable place to the ego. Husserl was right to emphasise the phenomenological aspect of the body, but he did so only on the basis of thinking the body from a specific point of view, namely that of a human standing on the earth. When the standpoint is switched, then the phenomenological method becomes questionable. Copernicus and the modern physicists who followed him considered the earth from a standpoint that is no longer on the earth but outside of it—a standpoint that was not yet phenomenologically valid. With the launch of the Sputnik and later the Apollo program, which were able to send back images of the 'blue marble' observed from outside, the situation radically changed. Hannah Arendt was very much aware of this when she declared in *The Human Condition* that this was the foremost scientific event of the twentieth century.[27]

Space exploration has definitively rendered the earth just one celestial body among many. The earth was considered by Buckminster Fuller as a spaceship, with humans as its passengers. The earth may have been an original ark upon which humans embarked, but now it is possible for humans to leave this ark, something which inspires great excitement: Mars is a potential alternative; as Elon Musk tells us on the website of SpaceX: 'I can't think of anything more exciting than going out there and being among the stars.' Although at present this remains a futuristic prospect, the view of the earth from outside has already rendered Husserl's standpoint only one possibility among others. In other words, the earth has ceased to be *Heimat*, and is henceforth only a spaceship.

A standpoint defines the direction of the gaze, but also limits it and affects the body to which the gaze belongs. Looking at world history from the standpoint of Japan, and vice versa, before and during the Second World War, a Japanese philosopher might be forgiven for having overemphasised the importance of Japan as a decisive moment

27. H. Arendt, *The Human Condition* (Chicago: Chicago University Press, 2002), 1.

in that world history. During the first symposium 'The Standpoint of World History and Japan' organised by the journal *Chūō Kōron* on 26 November 1941, Keiji Nishitani lamented Europeans' inability to look at the world from a different standpoint: 'In general Europeans, even now, seem to me to be unable to shake their habit of always viewing the world from a European perspective [見地].'[28] According to Nishitani, Europe perceived a crisis without knowing that this crisis emerged out of the collapse of the relation that it had maintained with the East. As the dialogue unfolds, Nishitani recalls that, on his way back to Japan from Germany, he was offered a book entitled *The Battlefront of the Coloured Race* by a man from Switzerland travelling on the same ship. Nishitani reports the conclusion of his reading as follows: '[O]ne of the most important consequences of this change [in reality] is that Europe is becoming merely one region among others.'[29] Wasn't this precisely what brought a sense of *Heimatlosigkeit* to Europe? And wasn't it this change of standpoint that allowed Nishitani to reclaim his own *Heimat* as, in a certain sense, post-Europe—as that which succeeds Europe as the centre of the world? As he says: '[T]he transformation now under way is the stuff of crisis for Europeans, while here it takes the form of a new world order. And when we discover that we are able to conceive of new concepts of world history and the philosophy of world history *here in Japan now* [現在日本で], this ability arises, I suspect, from the [very] gap in consciousness about which I have been speaking.'[30]

28. D. Williams, *The Philosophy of Japanese Wartime Resistance: A Reading, with Commentary, of the Complete Texts of the Kyoto School Discussions of 'The Standpoint of World History and Japan'* (London: Routledge, 2014), 115; see also K. Nishitani, M. Kosaka, S. Suzuki, I. Koyama, *The Standpoint of World History and Japan* (『世界史的立場 と日本』)(Tokyo: Chūō Kōron, 1943), 11.

29. Ibid., 118. The translation continues as follows: '... instead of the region that dominates the rest. Europe is ceasing to be the world', but this 'complementary' part is not to be found in the Japanese original; see *The Standpoint of World History and Japan*, 15.

What we hear in these symposiums of the Kyoto School philosophers is that Europe's loss of centrality in the world is taken to imply also the prominence of Japan as agent of world history.[31] In other words, Japan's significance can only be seen from the standpoint of a world history in which the world spirit has already departed from Europe owing to its decline, as witnessed by Oswald Spengler and many others. However, we might want to ask whether Japan was not also disoriented in this process of modernisation—that is to say, whether its becoming the centre of East Asia was not also something *unheimlich*. It didn't seem so to Nishitani, but we or the next generation may be able to analyse it differently. In order to compete with Europe to be the centre of the world or to be the world itself, Japan had to undergo a more intensified process of modernisation so as to catch up and surpass the European nations. The 'inferiority' of Japan or Asian countries in general to Europe could only be sublated through the reorientation of Japan from the standpoint of world history, a world history evaluated from

30. Williams, *The Philosophy of Japanese Wartime Resistance*, 116; see also *The Standpoint of World History and Japan*, 12.

31. Yoshimi Takeuchi, in his book *Overcoming Modernity* (1959), attempted to analyse a 'dual structure of the Greater East Asia War', which is at the same time a war against Western imperialism and a war of colonial invasion, see Y. Takeuchi, *Overcoming Modernity* (近代の超克) (Tokyo: Chikuma Shobō, 1983), 83; Wataru Hiromatsu on the other hand, in his *On 'Overcoming Modernity': A Perspective on the History of Shōwa Thought* (「近代の超克」論—昭和思想史への一視角) (Tokyo: Kōdansha, 1989), replied that the Kyoto School thinkers wanted to overcome modernity from a culturalist point of view and undermine the question of capitalism, especially Japan's turn toward a state monopoly capitalism. Many notable Japanese thinkers, including Masao Maruyama and Kojin Karatani, participated in this discussion, which is yet to be sufficiently evaluated. For a historical survey in English, see N. Matsui, '"Overcoming Modernity," Capital, and Life System: Divergence of "Nothing" in the 1970s and 1980s', *Journal of East Asian Philosophy* (2023).

the standpoint of Japan. There is a paradox at play here, since it was this same process of modernisation that gave Japan (as well as other East Asian countries) confidence to enter onto the stage of world history but also produced a *ressentiment* of *Heimatlosigkeit*, which resulted in a persisting antagonism between East and West in the East Asian psyche. What we have here is yet another process of dis-orientation.

In 1941 Nishitani envisioned a 'post-Europe' whose existence would later be pronounced from within by Jan Patočka: after the Second World War, Europe ceased to be the world power.[32] In recognising this fact, Nishitani wanted to elevate Japan to the status of the main protagonist of the world history, one that emerges in light of the decline of the West, while Patočka, like Heidegger, would seek to go back to the ancient Greeks, although rather than the question of Being, he sought an answer in Plato's doctrine of the care of the soul. But was Nishitani's analysis of the decline of Europe accurate? Or did a misjudgment of it lead to a profound disorientation that he himself failed to grasp? Nothing is more ironic than when we compare what Nishitani said about the Second World War with what Heidegger later analysed as the end of philosophy. Recall Heidegger's famous verdict in his 1964 'The End of Philosophy and the Task of Thinking':

> The end of philosophy proves to be the triumph of the manipulable arrangement of a scientific-technological world and of the social order proper to this world. The end of philosophy means: the beginning of the world civilization based upon Western European thinking.[33]

32. J. Patočka, *Europa und Nach-Europa: Zur Phänomenologie einer Idee* (Baden-Baden: Karl Alber, 2020).

33. M. Heidegger, *On Time and Being*, tr. J. Stambaugh (New York: Harper & Row, 1972), 59.

This contrast reveals something *unheimlich*. The new world order that Nishitani and other Kyoto School thinkers talked about, and which was used to justify the moral obligation of Japan to invade other Asian countries upon gaining self-consciousness of its own place in world history, is nothing but the continuation of Western European thinking. It would be curious to know what Nishitani would have had to say about Heidegger's assertion. Surely world history seen from the standpoint of Japan awakened by European or more precisely German historicism continues to be the unfolding of the Western Geist. In other words, *Heimat* is that which manifests itself like a mirage emerging from the desert of *Heimatlosigkeit*.

However, when one looks at the world from the standpoint of *Heimatlosigkeit*, something is opened up in an uncanny way, because there is no longer a home, fixed identity is sublated, and history and place are charged with new meanings. The ideology of *Heimat* as a fixed time and place reveals itself to be reactionary, in the sense that it cannot negate the planetary condition. It can only reproduce a politics of nostalgia and exclusion. Confrontation with the Other and freedom of movement reproduce the ideology of *Heimat*. This doesn't mean that we consider planetarisation as something desirable, but rather that, as a historical consequence, it cannot be completely negated. However, we have to overcome it. And to overcome planetarisation is to re-orient ourselves, in order to redefine a locality or a situatedness. Indeed, one of the major failures of the twentieth century was the inability to articulate the relation between locality and technology, and a reliance upon an almost standardised ecological thinking endowed with a strong European humanism; technology was received as a provocation to either a reactionary politics based on a dualism between tradition and modernity, or a fanatical accelerationism which believes that the problems that we have inherited will finally be resolved by technological advancement, whether it be geoengineering for repairing the earth or the subversion of capitalism by accelerating toward full automation. From the economic and technocratic perspective, there is very little value in taking locality into consideration besides its relevance to the availability of natural resources or other potential economic values.

It is clear that, for Heidegger, to overcome doesn't mean to negate. Instead, it means to look for another path which bypasses the framework of planetarisation. The homecoming of Heidegger to ancient Greece was an attempt to retrieve the question of Being. This questioning however also prevents Heidegger's thinking from opening to the Other. One steps back in order to move forward; however, such a stepping back is also a distancing from the Other. Even though Heidegger became interested in Daoism and Buddhism through his Japanese students, he refused the idea that looking to the East could afford the possibility of overcoming modernity, since for him to overcome modernity meant first of all to adopt an orientation toward *Heimat*. In so doing, Heidegger became a 'state thinker', as did his disciples such as Keiji Nishitani and Alexander Dugin.

One might contest that Heidegger is not a state thinker but a thinker of the people. We will have to make a distinction here: a state thinker is one who takes the state as the absolute for the people, that is to say, one for whom without the state there is no people; a thinker of the people is one who reactivates the historical resources sedimented among the people in order to call for and welcome a new becoming. We leave it to the reader to judge which kind of thinker Heidegger is. But more importantly, perhaps we have to confront the following question: *How can one avoid becoming a state thinker; can one avoid it at all?* It was the hero who founded the city in ancient Greece, and to become a state thinker is to yield to the temptation of such a heroic act; even the wise Plato couldn't resist returning to Syracuse twice to persuade Dionysius II to realise his theory concerning laws and government, even though his first visit to Syracuse ended up in unfortunate circumstances, when he was sold as slave by Dionysius I, the father of Dionysius II, as we are told in the *Seventh Letter*. The state needs thinkers, thinkers need the state, and therefore thinkers become the thinkers of *Heimat* because *Heimat* legitimates the state as the organism of the people.

A state thinker elevates their *Heimat* above other places in the world and attempts to seize the decisive moment of historical development from its standpoint—the unification of philosophy and power. In past centuries, almost every philosopher was addressed according to nationality, and a new school of thought was often prefixed with a nationality. A thinker can only go beyond the nation state by becoming *heimatlos*, that is to say, by looking at the world from the standpoint of not being at home. This doesn't mean that one must refrain from talking or thinking about a particular place or a culture—on the contrary, one must confront it and access it from the perspective of a planetary future.

Heimatlosigkeit becomes a standpoint from which to reflect on the planetary condition, and world history can only be reviewed from the standpoint of *Heimatlosigkeit*. One nation can no longer be said to be ahead of others in the journey of the world spirit; instead, philosophical reason must address the planetary condition and therefore become planetary. But in this case, not being at home is at the same time being at home, since home and not being at home are not opposed to one another. Not being at home means being somewhere else; being somewhere else doesn't have to be opposed to being at home. Instead, not being at home allows one to know better both being at home and being in the world.

CHAPTER ONE

PHILOSOPHY and POST-EUROPE

Will Europe become *what it is in reality*—that is, a little promontory on the continent of Asia? Or will it remain *what it seems*—that is, the elect portion of the terrestrial globe, the pearl of the sphere, the brain of a vast body?

—Paul Valéry[1]

What makes Europe—that is philosophy ... Philosophy is European in an intrinsic way, and it could definitely be said, precisely in the European tradition of the term, 'in an essential way'. But I will not say this, and this non-use of the term 'essential' or of any reference to being also means, in this case, that philosophy is henceforth called upon to become global, alongside the technology that has left Europe to expand across all the other continents—a development contemplated by Valéry. For the European necessity of philosophy is techno-logical. Which is to say, hypermnesic. And accidental precisely in this respect.

—Bernard Stiegler[2]

How should we think of this statement, written by Bernard Stiegler after the death of his mentor Jacques Derrida in 2004, regarding the future of European philosophy and its relation to technology? We are reminded here that 'philosophy is European in a strict sense', as Derrida said in Shanghai three years before his death—more precisely, on the 11th of September 2001, the day when Derrida arrived in Shanghai and was received by his hosts at the French Embassy.[3] It is reported that during the reception, Derrida said to his Chinese

1. P. Valéry, 'The Crisis of the Mind', in *Valéry: An Anthology*, ed. J.R. Lawler (London and Henley: Routledge and Kegan Paul, 1977), 102.
2. B. Stiegler, 'The Magic Skin; or, The Franco-European Accident of Philosophy after Jacques Derrida', *Qui Parle: Critical Humanities and Social Sciences* 18:1 (2009): 99.

colleagues: 'China didn't have philosophy, but only thought.'[4] We don't know whether Derrida used the present tense or the past tense here, since in Chinese there is no tense, no time imposed on the verb, and therefore perhaps no historicity in a teleological sense. In any case, Derrida produced another shock among his Chinese hosts, in addition to the collapse of the twin towers in New York on the same day. Twenty years later, Derrida's verdict continues to haunt Chinese intellectuals.

§3. The Spirit of European Philosophy

There is no doubt that philosophy is European: not only that it is a Greek term, the love of wisdom, but also that philosophy in the European sense is, first of all, a philosophy of Being, a thinking of essence. Derrida consoled his Chinese hosts by humbly declaring that he didn't mean to depreciate Chinese thought, and that his remark simply reflected the fact that philosophy was born historically in Greece, and carries within itself a trajectory and a destiny which is strictly speaking European. In other words, Greece is

3. 'Borradori: Where were you on September 11? Derrida: I was in Shanghai, at the end of a long trip to China. It was nighttime there, and the owner of the cafe I was in with a couple of friends came to tell us that an airplane had "crashed" into the Twin Towers. I hurried back to my hotel, and from the very first televised images, those of CNN, I note, it was easy to foresee that this was going to become, in the eyes of the world, what you called a "major event". Even if what was to follow remained, to a certain extent, invisible and unforeseeable. But to feel the gravity of the event and its "worldwide" implications it was enough simply to mobilize a few already tested political hypotheses.' G. Borradori, *Philosophy in a Time of Terror: Dialogues with Jürgen Habermas and Jacques Derrida* (Chicago: University of Chicago Press, 2004), 109–10.

4. Y. Wang (王元化), 'Talks about Philosophy and Culture of Chinese and Western' (关于中西哲学与文化的对话), *Journal of Literature, History and Philosophy* (《文史哲》) 2 (2002): 5–8.

the *Heimat* of philosophy; and Novalis was perhaps right that philosophy, in so far as it is European, is driven by its homesickness, namely its constant return to the question of Being. For the question of Being shaped the mode of philosophical inquiry of what is called the Occident today. In this tradition, Being is revealed through *logos*, and therefore we can understand the term logocentrism without any negative connotations. This theoretical effort to grasp Being as such and in its totality, according to Edmund Husserl, distinguishes European philosophy or Greco-European science from other so-called philosophies of India and China. The former is grounded in theory, the latter in practice; the former progresses towards the universal, while the latter are limited to the local—making them thought, but not philosophy. Maybe we might even say that the universal qua rational is what Husserl characterises as the spiritual figure of Europe:

'The spiritual figure of Europe'—what is it? It is exhibiting the philosophical idea immanent in the history of Europe (of spiritual Europe). To put it another way, it is its immanent teleology, which, if we consider mankind in general, manifests itself as a new human epoch emerging and beginning to grow, the epoch of a humanity that from now on will and can live only in the free fashioning of its being and its historical life out of rational ideas and infinite tasks.[5]

5. E. Husserl, 'Philosophy and the Crisis of European Man', lecture in Vienna, 10 May 1935, <https://www.hs-augsburg.de/~harsch/germanica/ Chronologie/20Jh/Husserl/hus_kris.html>: '«Die geistige Gestalt Europas»— was ist das? Die der Geschichte Europas (des geistigen Europas) immanente philosophische Idee aufzuweisen, oder, was dasselbe ist, die ihr immanente Teleologie, die sich vom Gesichtspunkt der universalen Menschheit überhaupt kenntlich macht als der Durchbruch und Entwicklungsanfang einer neuen Menschheitsepoche, der Epoche der Menschheit, die nunmehr bloß leben will und leben kann in der freien Gestaltung ihres Daseins, ihres historischen Lebens aus Ideen der Vernunft, aus unendlichen Aufgaben.'

Husserl tells us that the spiritual figure [*Gestalt*] of Europe is tele-
ologically driven by the pursuit of rationality; this teleology is not
only European, but rather concerns humanity in general. According
to Husserl, the crisis of the European spirit owes to its decline into
naturalism and objectivism; the phenomenological method stands
as a candidate to resecure European science, rescuing it from its
decadence. This decadence, more precisely, owes to a technicisation
[*Technisierung*] of knowledge which bypasses all noetic activities. It
is not our question today to judge whether Husserl's solution still
holds; what interests us here is how *logos* constitutes the principle of
European thought. Derrida and Stiegler use *technē* to deconstruct
this European Ideal of logocentrism, as well as Husserl's phenomenology, demonstrating that logos is unsustainable without *technē*,
and that *idealisation*, in so far as it is not mere *ideation*, exists only
in a technical form.[6] Therefore, both Derrida and Stiegler add to
Husserl's claim that philosophy is essentially European the addi-
tional claim that this is not only because of the pursuit of theoretical
logos, but also because this pursuit necessarily demands the support of *technē*.[7] The relation between *logos* and *technē* is *essentially*

6. According to Stiegler, the distinction could be made as follows: ideation is
   the making-present of something in the mind, for example, when we think of
   a triangle; idealisation is the condition under which such ideation is possible,
   for example, we learn what a triangle is by looking at the externalised figure.
7. This could be also read as the deconstruction of Western metaphysics,
   because metaphysics presupposes the opposition between *logos* and *technē*,
   intelligible and sensible. See B. Stiegler, *Technics and Time 1: The Fault of
   Epimetheus* (Stanford, CA: Stanford University Press, 1998), 185–86:
   '[S]ince metaphysics is constituted through the very formation of an opposition between *logos* and *tekhnē*, *phusis* and *nomos*, the intelligible and the
   sensible, asters and disasters, haps and mishaps. Thus, for metaphysics: (1)
   tekhnē, the field of artifacts, is the possibility of the arbitrary and of the worst
   hubris, of the violence of man against *phusis* when he considers himself a god;
   and (2) the logos, the site of *alētheia*, is also the *metron*, in the attention that
   it brings to the "as such" of a being (to its *phusis*).'

anamnesic, since technics is the support of memory and thinking; it is the externalisation of memory and that which allows internalisation as remembering or recollecting. Adding to Derrida's caricature of European philosophy as logocentrism, Stiegler supplements it with a *techno-logocentrism*. These two thinkers then deconstruct the history of Western metaphysics through the reconstitution of a theory of *techno-logos*.

Secondly, and paradoxically, this essence of European philosophy is also *accidental*, since technology is accidental to the European *logos* according to Stiegler, who presents technology as essential accident or accidental necessity. In Greek mythology, this accidental nature of technology was expressed in the original fault of Epimetheus and the second fault of Prometheus as compensation and supplement, as told in Hesiod's *Works and Days* and *Theogony*, and in Plato's *Protagoras*.[8] This mythological origin of technology in European culture lies in the fault of the titan Epimetheus, who forgot to distribute skills to the human as he had done to all other living beings; and it consequently led to the fault of his brother Prometheus, who stole fire from the Olympian gods to give a quality to the qualityless human species who stood naked in the forest waiting to be torn apart by animals. This fault became a *default*, a necessity, or, as Stiegler puts it, *le defaut qu'il faut*, namely the becoming-necessity of the accident. The *mise-en-scène* of the mythology of Prometheus and Epimetheus as witness to the birth of European philosophy reveals the intimate relation between *logos* and *technē* and the particularity of this relation. If philosophy is intrinsically European, it is because the European spirit is the history of *techno-logos*. European philosophy is contingent, yet it is also that which makes such contingency necessary, universal, and ideal. This historical process is teleological because it demands a self-consciousness of the spirit. This was already made clear by Hegel, who was able to theorise the absolute spirit by interpreting these accidents as the necessary medium of the coming of the absolute—the cunning of reason.

8. See *The Question Concerning Technology in China*, 7–18 [§1].

In his early article 'Persephone, Oedipus and Epimetheus' (1992), Stiegler showed that Plato's *Meno* in a way anticipates the problem of eideticity in relation to consciousness as posed by Husserl in his *Logical Investigations*. Recall the famous *aporia* in Plato's *Meno*, in which Socrates was challenged by *Meno*: if he, Socrates, already knows what virtue is, then he has no need to inquire after it; while if he doesn't know what virtue is, then even if he encountered it, he would not be able to recognise it. That is to say, one will never know exactly what virtue is, since there is a *temporal difference* between knowing and an object of knowledge such as virtue. Socrates replied with the ruse that he knew, but had forgotten after the incarnation of the soul, so that now he can *remember* it. Socrates demonstrates this process of 'recollection' (*anamnesis*) by asking an uneducated slave boy to resolve a geometrical problem by drawing on the sand. Commenting on this aporia, Stiegler writes:

> An eidetic vision of virtue in general is the condition of the experience of a particular virtue. Virtue as such does not exist. Only virtues in the particular exist. And yet, without the 'irreality' of virtue, no 'real' virtues would appear. Without existing itself, virtue consists in, and insists through, the series of all existent virtues. It haunts the series: it is a ghost, a spirit.[9]

In other words, if real virtue can only be accessed through anamnesis, the process of anamnesis demands a memory support: the young slave is taught by Socrates to resolve a geometrical problem by tracing lines on the sand—an *externalisation* of his memory and an *internalisation* through recollection or anamnesis. Here lies a particular relation between European philosophy and technology, according to Stiegler: European philosophy was the consequence of an accident, and its development is fundamentally an *anamnesis* which consists

---

9. B. Stiegler, 'Persephone, Oedipus, Epimetheus', tr. R. Beardsworth, *Technema* 3 (1996): 70.

in making this accident necessary; but now, for European philosophy to continue to survive in the age of globalisation, it will have to recognise its accidental techno-logical nature, and constitute *a new hypermnesic condition*. In this sense, we would be more justified in saying that technology—*techno-logos*—is not simply about craft making or machine building—after all, the Chinese, the Japanese, the Persians, and the Indians also had these things—but rather that it designates the systematic movement via which European *Geist* was only able to become conscious of itself and the necessity of its movement via its techno-scientific exteriorisation.

Thus authors such as Husserl, Valéry, and Patočka, writing in the twentieth century about the crisis of Europe, somehow take up the Hegelian concept of spirit, which as Derrida noted is nothing traditional, but rather modern.[10] If this spirit is fundamentally that of *techno-logos*, as affirmed by Stiegler, then we must also understand that the globalisation we have witnessed is only a continued colonisation on the part of this spirit, and we must then also admit that a true dialogue, or what I prefer to call an *individuation of thinking*, has not yet taken place; past efforts can only be considered as *reflections* of Europe upon itself. The philosophical and technological system that the moderns inherit today is *essentially* European and *accidentally* American. This inheritance is achieved through hundreds of years of colonisation, modernisation, and globalisation of its industrial capitalism. Today we are in an epoch of disorientation (the subtitle of the second volume of *Technics and Time*),[11] but it is not only a loss of orientation, but also a dis-orient-ation, a loss of the Orient and of the Occident.

However, if technology has already left Europe and expanded to the rest of the world, is it still European? And if so, is Europe a geographical region, a people, or a spirit? Or could we say that

---

10. Derrida, *The Other Heading*, 27.
11. B. Stiegler, *Technics and Time 2. Disorientation*, tr. S. Barker (Stanford, CA: Stanford University Press, 2008).

technology never left Europe, but just extended from Europe to the entire globe? To return to Stiegler, if we correctly understand what he said, philosophy remains European because technological thought is still and essentially European. It is European technology that has made possible a European philosophy, made philosophy European, and made European philosophy global. Europe's capacity for universalisation very clearly owes not to its theoretical advancement, but to the fact that, in the European modern era, technological advancement, especially in marine power and military technology, made Europe a stronger force in comparison to non-European lands.

This externalisation [*Entäusserung*, or alienation] is the medium through which the spirit is able to know itself. Only by knowing itself is it capable of projecting into the future, in terms of both rationality and effective means. Hegel was probably one of the first European thinkers to recognise the necessity of the objective spirit, which serves both as the other of the subjective spirit and as its tertiary retention (in Stiegler's sense), so that an *Er-innerung* is possible, so that the spirit can march toward the absolute. This triad of the subjective, the objective, and the absolute constitutes the dynamic of the journey of the spirit, which culminates in various milestones in art, religion, and philosophy. The European spirit progresses through the externalisation in and internalisation of technology, and therefore Stiegler is able to claim that it was only in Hegel that the concept of historicity became possible.[12] Outside of Europe there have been histories, both in oral and written forms, but there may not have been historicity in the sense that Heidegger attributes to this term. That is to say, even though in these cultures and civilisations one can also find technologies, that doesn't mean that the relation between spirit and technology is the same or that the journey of the spirit is driven by the same motivation and oriented by the same procedures. Nishitani once commented that he had the

---

12. See the interview with Stiegler in the film *The Ister* (dir. David Barison and
    Daniel Ross, 2004).

impression that in Eastern cultures such as India, China, and Japan, there is a lack of understanding of historicity in Heidegger's sense, although for sure one can find all kinds of historiographies in these non-European cultures:

> I am sure that Buddhism falls short of such historical conscious-ness, at least to some extent. Generally speaking, something called 'historical' exists no less in China than in India and Japan. But I have the impression that in these countries there has been no trace of seeing the world as history in the true sense of the word. [...] [T]his way of thinking is somewhat dif-ferent from an historical one, at least of the sort prevalent in the modern world.[13]

There are two negations or refusals in this comment. Firstly, Nishitani states that Asian cultures to date have not developed a historical con-sciousness, and that they therefore haven't been able to understand themselves from the standpoint of world history and consequently to comprehend world history from their own standpoint. There is a different conception of time in Europe and in Asia. The second refusal consists in a paradox: there is writing in these cultures, so why wasn't a historical consciousness developed? In the symposium 'The Standpoint of World History and Japan', we find a discussion of exactly the same puzzle among the Kyoto School historians and philosophers. There, one of the participants, Masaaki Kosaka, makes the following observation:

> I have been looking at the ways in which recent European and Chinese historians have addressed their work. It is my impression that Europeans and Chinese take radically differ-ent approaches to the study of the past. European historians

---

13. K. Nishitani, *On Buddhism*, tr. S. Yamamoto and R.E. Carter (New York: SUNY Press, 2006), 40.

develop a steady stream of different ideas and themes. This pattern is very evident in their writings. But when one turns to books by Chinese historians, there appears to be comparatively little development of ideas or themes. Rather, one topic after another is raised only suddenly to disappear. An era ends, and so does the story. Rulers come and go, and there the discussion ends.[14]

In other words, there has been only historiography, without historical consciousness. This might be because the heaven reigns, and in so far as the mandate of the heaven is what counts the most, then it would appear immediately meaningless to ponder upon the meaning of history. But this paradox should be disturbing for Stiegler, because it implies that there might be *no necessary relation* between tertiary retention (e.g. writing) and historicity, as implied by the Japanese thinkers' remarks about the presence of historiography and the absence of historicity in China and Japan; more speculatively, it leads one to wonder whether there might be technics that escape *techno-logos*, that is, technics whose mode of anamnesis is different from the Platonic one.[15] There is then a tension between the universal dimension of technics that Stiegler analysed in terms of tertiary retention, and the specificity of the kind of historical view that is developed by Hegel and runs through the works of Nietzsche, Heidegger, Derrida, and Stiegler himself.[16]

14. Williams, *The Philosophy of Japanese Wartime Resistance*, 126.
15. This might well be the question that Jean-François Lyotard raised in his seminar titled 'Logos and Technē, or Telegraphy', when invited by Bernard Stiegler in 1986. The seminar was later published in J.-F. Lyotard, *The Inhuman: Reflections on Time*, tr. G. Bennington and R. Bowlby (Stanford, CA: Stanford University Press, 1991). At the end of the text, Lyotard mentioned the Zen Buddhist Dōgen's 'broken mirror' as an example of an anamnesis that transcends the industrial hegemony on memory. Stiegler remarked to me several times that this part on Dōgen was 'bizarre'.

§4. The CONSTITUTION of POST-EUROPE

One may argue that, although it still exists as a political unit
through the formation of the European Union, today Europe is
fundamentally *fragmented*, as we can see in the differences between
countries within the European Union, as well as between EU countries and those not yet integrated into the EU political unit, or
which are now deciding to leave. The eastern European countries
distinguish themselves from the western European countries, and
sometimes consider themselves as postcolonial subjects: to the eyes
of non-Europeans, they are part of the colonial power, while they
see themselves as being colonised by Western Europe. Therefore,
any claim about European philosophy must first of all recognise
its multiplicity, and the irreducibility of the different ways of thinking within European philosophy. There has been Greek philosophy,
German philosophy, French philosophy, British philosophy, however, they are all manifestations of the European spirit. This is why
Valéry, Husserl, and Patočka were able to talk about the crisis of
the European spirit and about Europe as an Idea. French philosophy is an accident of the spiritual life of Europe, as Stiegler said,
because it is the appropriation of something non-French, namely
German philosophy, Kant, Hegel, Nietzsche, Heidegger, etc.;
however, what makes French philosophy necessary (in all its accidentality) to the history of philosophy is its capacity (especially
in the school of Derrida) to render explicit the role of technology
in the European spirit.

If the essence of French philosophy does not lie in its being a
nationalist philosophy, it is because, in comparison with its German
precursor, it was able to take the European spirit further than its
contemporaries. It is a singularity of the development of European

16. This is a subject that I tried to analyse in *The Question Concerning Technology in
China*, where I attempted to show that Chinese thought has a different understanding of categories such as nature, technology, and time.

philosophy, and this singularity comes out of a process of individuation.[17] However, French philosophy might well become a nationalist philosophy, if it should fail to individuate in the future. That is to say, it may end up defending a Frenchness that exists only as mere national identity.

Now, in order for European philosophy to have a future, if Europe is to continue to be philosophical, according to Stiegler's diagnosis, then it will have to seize upon the techno-logical accident of its globalisation. Directly after the passage cited in the epigraph to this chapter, Stiegler continues:

> In short, Europe is called to a global becoming (to exist on a global scale) *with* its philosophy—*failing which it will die*—and can become so only by 'de-Europeanizing' itself. It will no longer remain in this world to come, it will have no future in other words, unless it is able *to turn its philosophy into something global*, and thereby stamp thought with the *intrinsically accidental* character of thought—and, furthermore, with the intrinsically *non-European* character of Europe and its future.[18]

However, isn't European philosophy already global? What does Stiegler mean to say when he speaks of turning philosophy into something global? And where is the globalised philosopher to find their *Heimat*? If we were to identify a latent anti-Eurocentrism in his thought, then maybe we could defend him in the following way: Stiegler is not making a claim for a homecoming of philosophy, because the *Heimat* is nothing but an accident; however, there has been a process that has rendered this accidental event necessary, and this process is the development of Western philosophy. Now, by recognising the accidentality of its origin, Europe will have to distance itself from the illusion of *Heimat* and demand a

---

17. We will elaborate on the 'individuation of thinking' in the next chapter.
18. Stiegler, 'The Magic Skin', 99.

de-Europeanisation. But what exactly would this mean? Would it mean becoming *heimatlos*? Or, in other words, would it mean becoming other, becoming like the Asian or the African?

The above quote ends with a reference to Marc Crépon's 2006 *Alterités de l'Europe*, without further comment. Like Derrida in *L'autre Cap* (1991), where he criticises any homogenealogy (of Europe) as mystification, in *Alterités de l'Europe* Crépon proposes to look at Europe from the perspective of alterity—that is to say, Europe is not a neat history passing from Greece to the Roman empire and then to Christianity.[19] This is a critique and a negotiation with Valéry, who, asking himself who the Europeans are, answered: 'I would consider as European all those peoples who, over the course of history, were subject to three influences', namely Rome, Greece, and Christianity. Instead, for Crépon, Europe contains an alterity which it aways attempts to deny, an alterity that is not even separable from Greece, Troy, Anatolia, etc. These non-European characteristics of Europe must be recognised, or must become conscious, as the condition of de-Europeanisation. This becoming-conscious or aware [*prise de conscience*] must be seen not only as an acknowledgement, but as what below we shall call *the condition of an individuation of thinking*.

In a chapter entitled 'Alterités de l'Europe' (the same as the book's title), Crépon engages with Jan Patočka's reflections on Europe, and highlights the danger of nationalism and totalitarianism which can be seen as being internal to Europe, as well as a Eurocentrism which insists on the universality of European rationality and exports it to the other. This universal rationality, Crépon argues, is a unidimensional and linear universality which was also the source of the crisis of the European spirit.[20]

Although Stiegler and Patočka share some similar interpretations of the crisis of the European spirit, they differ fundamentally in their

---

19. M. Crépon, *Altérités de l'Europe* (Paris: Galilée, 2006), 21. Note that the introduction of this book is dedicated to Bernard Stiegler.

understanding of the role played by technology in European spiritual life. Patočka questioned at points whether techno-civilisation is decadent; he then tried to demonstrate, throughout a whole chapter of his *Heretical Essays* (1975), that this is indeed so, although in the end he remained ambivalent and undecisive. Indeed, as we shall see later, Patočka's understanding of technology oscillates between Husserl's critique of European science and Heidegger's critique of *Gestell*. In the *Heretical Essays*, even though he recognises that the techno-civilisation 'makes possible more than any previous human constellation: a life without violence and with far-reaching equality of opportunity',[21] and admits that the question of whether techno-civilisation is decadent or not is perhaps not a correctly posed question, Patočka sees the emergence of modern science and technology as the turning point in the decline of European reason:

20. It is not uninteresting to note that in an article published in the German newspaper *FAZ* (2003) by Jürgen Habermas and co-signed by Jacques Derrida, intended as a response to the United States' war in Iraq and European political leaders' call for a Europe unity with the US, Habermas called for the autonomy of Europe against the unilateral foreign policy of the US. Toward the end of the text, Habermas proposed that the European powers 'assume a reflective distance from themselves', a distance that would allow them to recognise the need to 'account for the violence of a forcible and uprooting process of modernization'. Habermas was pointing out that Europe must develop a 'strategic autonomy', as Emmanuel Macron would claim twenty years later after his visit to China in 2023. However, it is very doubtful whether today such an autonomy of foreign policy is sufficient to address the planetary condition, or whether it only follows again the good old European *nomos* of the earth, in Carl Schmitt's sense. See J. Habermas and J. Derrida, 'February 15, or What Binds Europeans Together: A Plea for a Common Foreign Policy, Beginning in the Core of Europe', in L. Thomassen (ed.), *The Derrida–Habermas Reader* (Edinburgh: Edinburgh University Press, 2006), 270–77.

21. J. Patočka, *Heretical Essays in the Philosophy of History*, tr. E. Kobak (Chicago: Open Court, 1996), 118.

The great turning point in the life of western Europe appears to be the sixteenth century. From that time on another motif comes to the fore, opposing the motif of the care of the soul and coming to dominate one area after another, politics, economics, faith, and science, transforming them in a new style. Not a care *for the soul*, the care to *be*, but rather the care to *have*, care for the external world and its conquest, becomes the dominant concern.[22]

Patočka returns to the 'care of the soul' in the Greek teaching as that which defines the fundamental question of European philosophy. There are two different figures [*Gestalten*] of care of the soul, Patočka argues: one (Democritus) searches for the totality of knowing, while the other (Socrates and Plato) seeks the highest development of the soul. The first, namely atomism, gives rise to a universal science which aims to overcome the errancy of the soul by pursuing the truth of things, while the second produces a doctrine of inner life, or philosophy.[23] Philosophy concerns the question of how to live, while knowing how to live is tantamount to knowing how to 'care for the soul'.[24] Post-Europe, according to Patočka, calls for a return to this foundation of philosophy which has been obscured and distracted by techno-scientific modernisation.

---

22. Ibid., 83.

23. J. Patočka, 'Europa und Nach-Europa. Die nacheuropäische Epoche und ihre geistigen Probleme', in *Ketzerische Essays zur Philosophie der Geschichte und ergänzende Schriften*, ed. K. Nellen and J. Němec (Stuttgart: Klett-Cotta, 1988), 287.

24. 'Our most important matter, πῶς βιώτεον (how to live), is only meaningful if what is essential in us, our being, is bound to it; and this essential core within us is the ψυχή (soul). That is why philosophy, whose task it is to explicitly pose, clarify, and treat the question of how we should live, can be defined as ἐπιμέλεια τῆς ψυχῆς, care for the soul, as is said in the *Apology*.' J. Patočka, 'On the Soul in Plato (1972)', in *The Selected Writings of Jan Patočka: Care for the Soul*, ed. E. Plunkett and I. Chvatík, tr. A. Zucker (London: Bloomsbury, 2022), 76.

For Patočka, post-Europe means first of all that, after the Second World War, Europe ceases to be the world power; this *Verlust* demands a reflection on the future of Europe and the overcoming of the decadence of its techno-civilisation. But this statement is rather ambivalent, because it could be equally read as eurocentric or anti-eurocentric: anti-eurocentric because it means that Europe is no longer the centre of the world, eurocentric because, for Patočka, there is 'no other history than European history'.[25] On the other hand, as a student and reader of Husserl, Patočka also adopts Husserl's critique of scientific rationality: post-Europe is a condition under which the life-world is increasingly reduced to objectivity and calculability.[26] Care of the soul stands as a candidate for a basic motif of a post-European philosophy, as Crépon summarises:

> The care for the soul implies no system of values referable to an authority or an institution, whatever it may be. On the contrary, if Patočka, in his reflection on the European heritage, is indeed in search of a 'unifying formative action', non-reducible to Europe's past domination, the care for the soul meets all the criteria required for such an action.[27]

The late Stiegler may have agreed upon the importance of caring since, for him, the question of *panser* (which Dan Ross translates as

---

25. 'Such a conception of history (and its corresponding philosophy of history) appears quite naïve and, moreover, dangerously Eurocentric.' K. Novotný, 'Europe, Post-Europe, and Eurocentrism', in *Thinking After Europe: Jan Patočka and Politics*, ed. F. Tava and D. Meacham (London: Rowman and Littlefield International, 2016), 301.

26. J. Patočka, 'Réflexion sur l'Europe', in *Liberté et Sacrifice. Écrits politiques* (Grenoble: Jérôme Million, 1993), 181–213.

27. M. Crépon, 'Fear, Courage, Anger: The Socratic Lesson', in *Jan Patočka and the Heritage of Phenomenology*, ed. I. Chvatík and E. Abrams (Dordrecht: Springer, 2011), 183.

'caring') is of ultimate importance, but for Stiegler, it is unthinkable without technology. Patočka understands that modern technology with its globalisation constitutes an exclusive reduction to what Kant calls understanding [*Verstand*][28] in contrast to self-reflective reason [*sich verstehende Vernunft*]. This criticism of technology resonates with Stiegler's criticism of contemporary digital technology, for the latter is capable of analytical power, but cannot be confused with reason in the Kantian sense.

In other words, we can say that for both Patočka and Stiegler, a post-European philosophy has to take technology seriously and to understand it radically.[29] However, there are fundamental differences between the two positions, and these differences could be seen as two subtle readings of Heidegger. The two key texts from Patočka on technology are found in a lecture given in September 1973, entitled 'The Dangers of Technicization in Science according to E. Husserl, and the Essence of Technology as Danger according to M. Heidegger' (also known as the Varna Lecture),[30] and in a seminar that followed in Prague in October 1973.[31] In this lecture Patočka compared Husserl's and Heidegger's reflections on technology, and aligned himself with the 'more radical' approach of Heidegger. Patočka understands Heidegger's diagnosis of the *Gestell* as a mode of comprehension which excludes other relations to Being, and sees in art a possibility of access to truth other than the *Gestell*: an other configuration of beings and the possibility of the unconcealment of Being. This reflection on art, which Heidegger himself explicitly

---

28. Novotný, 'Europe, Post-Europe, and Eurocentrism', 303.
29. Marcia Sá Cavalcante Schuback suggests that the question of technology is central to Patočka's philosophy, see M. Sá Cavalcante Schuback, 'Sacrifice and Salvation: Jan Patočka's Reading of Heidegger on the Question of Technology', in Chvatík and Abrams (eds.), *Jan Patočka and the Heritage of Phenomenology*, 23–37.
30. See Patočka, *The Selected Writings*, 281–94.
31. See Patočka, *Liberté et sacrifice*, 277–324.

referred to in *The Origin of the Work of Art* (1935/36) and *The Question Concerning Technology* (1949/1953), is considered by Patočka as *das Rettende*—the 'saving power' of which Hölderlin spoke. However, neither art nor philosophical reflection are able to undertake the necessary profound transformation.[32] What is primordial for Patočka is the return to the soul, and to the classics in which the soul stands as the condition of possibility of philosophy, of truth. Philosophy, unlike art, doesn't involve full participation, as in dance, but rather demands distance: 'a distancing that realises that everything is a mystery. It is from this mystery that the question arises—"What is it?"—the meaning of which will be the subject of philosophical reflection.'[33] The negativity of modern technology necessitates a distance, which Patočka calls sacrifice. The saving power lies in resistance to the temptation of technological totalisation, in favour of a clearing for the ground of appearing.

> Can we, however, understand this great upheaval which, historically manifests itself in the readiness of ever so many to sacrifice themselves for the sake of a different, better world simply in terms of a will to arrange oneself within what is manageable, within our power and calculation? [...] [A] sacrifice means precisely drawing back from the real of what can be managed and ordered, and an explicit relation to which, not being anything actual itself, serves as the ground of the appearing of all that is active and in that sense rules over all.[34]

This might sound like what is called 'degrowth' today, although the theory of degrowth doesn't concern the question of Being. At least

---

32. Patočka, 'The Dangers of Technicization in Science', 285.

33. 'Une distanciation qui se rend compte que tout es un mystère. C'est du mystère que surgit la question—«qu'est ce que c'est»—dont le sens fera l'objet de la réflection philosophique.' Patočka, *Liberté et sacrifice*, 290–91.

34. Patočka, 'The Dangers of Technicization in Science', 290.

we can say that, through sacrifice, a new relation between human and technology will appear.

For Stiegler, on the other hand, the 'saving power' is to be found, paradoxically, in technology itself. Stiegler's gesture is tragist, in the sense that it aims to *overcome Gestell via technology*, as Nietzsche wanted to do with nihilism—and art is an appropriation of technology by turning it into something extraordinary. Stiegler, to some degree, then, agrees with Patočka on his assessment of art, and on the extraordinary to be found in the work of art; but he does not agree that returning to the soul or to art alone will resolve the problem. For Stiegler, the primordial question of philosophy is not the soul but rather technology, for the soul itself is a *technoesis*, since in so far it is possible, *noesis* depends on a memory support without which it would not be able to think. If *das Rettende* really exists, it is, paradoxically, to be found in technology.

In other words, technology is the central question of a post-European philosophy. A post-European philosophy cannot be sustained if it fails to take the question of technology as its provenance and its future. Heidegger was clear on this point since technology is central to his thought, and it is even more explicit in the thinking of Stiegler,[35] while for Patočka, caring for the soul is something that 'in its very essence is not technological [...] not merely instrumental'.[36] This remains a blind spot in Patočka's thinking of Post-Europe and in his diagnosis of technology.[37] As we said earlier, the difference between Stiegler and Patočka lies in their respective conceptions of the future of Europe and its relation to technology. This fundamental difference might be analysed by going back to the elementary question of geometry. In *Plato and Europe*, Patočka pointed out that geometrical elements such as a line or a circle,

---

35. Novotný, 'Europe, Post-Europe, and Eurocentrism', 305.

36. J. Patočka, 'The Obligation to Resist Injustice', in *Philosophy and Selected Writings*, ed., tr. E. Kohák (Chicago: Chicago University Press, 1989); also quoted in Crépon, 'Fear, Courage, Anger: The Socratic Lesson', 183.

defined as something without thickness, do not exist in the world. Patočka found the response in the specific place of mathematics in the anatomy of the soul:

> We have numbers, lines, surfaces, stereometric bodies within the domain of mathematics. Four geometric spatial representations in total. But these four spatial representations are simultaneously, vertically conceived, the model of the hierarchy of existence: at the bottom the material world, then the mathematical, which mediates between the material world and the higher one, and finally the archetypes of the linking of the indeterminate and unity—these are the *ideas*. The mathematical is continuous with the ideas, and this *mathematical* is at the same time the soul.[38]

The mathematical, or number, is that which mediates between the world of things and the world of ideas. However, according to Stiegler, phenomenology still failed to resolve the question of the ideality of a point, a line, or a circle: phenomenology at most stays on the level of *ideation* but falls short of idealisation. Through the

37. Patočka's phenomenological critique of Europe continues in more recent literature, for example, Corine Pelluchon's *Les Lumières à l'âge du vivant* (Paris: Seuil, 2022), where, after a criticism of technology and transhumanism via Günther Anders, Bernard Stiegler, and Gilbert Simondon (chapter 5), Pelluchon returns to Patočka's imaginary of a Post-Europe (chapter 6), one that gives up pursuing the 'external path of conquest and universal hegemony' and instead takes an 'internal path of the opening of the planet as opening of the world'. Pelluchon's proposal for a 'new Enlightenment' is brave and encouraging. However, a return to Patočka's 'taking care of the soul' without a deconstruction of its relation to technology is the Achilles' heel of such a project for a 'New Enlightenment'.

38. J. Patočka, *Plato and Europe*, tr. P. Lom (Stanford, CA: Stanford University Press, 2002), 102.

example of the slave boy being able to draw in the sand in order to resolve a geometrical problem in Plato's *Meno*, Stiegler claims that *idealisation* always demands a technical supplement, a means of anamnesis. A point by definition is without dimension. However, we have never experienced such a thing, nor have we ever seen a line which has only one dimension. The point and the line can only be thought through something other than their definitions—for example, when the slave boy draws a line in the sand, it is already a two-dimensional surface. Patočka also remarked that Democritus was able to get from the visible to the invisible by 'sketching a geometrical form in the sand',[39] but despite this Patočka bypassed the question of technology and went directly to the care of the soul. We might say that Patočka remains a Husserlian par excellence in his diagnosis of the problem of Europe as well as in his response, while Stiegler looks at phenomenology and Europe after Derrida's deconstruction of Husserl's 'Origin of Geometry'. However, it is not our task to deconstruct Patočka, but rather to understand what is at stake in the concept of Post-Europe.

Stiegler sees that *techno-logos* is European par excellence, and offers Europe the possibility of pursuing a new opportunity in the process of globalisation. However, when the European spirit and its superiority and domination is invoked, one risks falling back either consciously or unconsciously into Eurocentrism. It remains to be asked what is the role that non-European cultures play in the becoming of the European Spirit. The European is essentially technological [*techno-logos*] and philosophical in the sense that it comes out of a necessary default, supplemented (compensated for) by technology, and the capacity to think about technology as both the possibility and necessity of the development of reason. If the non-European is considered to be outside of reason, as Hegel said of Siberia in his lectures on *The Philosophy of History*,[40] then the non-European, even if they have some 'pre-modern' technology, is not able to participate in

39. Ibid., 115.

the European spirit, since they have no role to play in the history of Spirit. Post-Europe in Patočka's sense could risk being a scenario in which the Other is only the Other of the self, not the absolute Other; as in the Hegelian dialectic, this Other will then be recognised as the Other of the self and finally sublated. This ambiguity can also be identified in Stiegler's thinking.

All of these readings risk assuming the world problem as a European problem, in which case Post Europe would simply mean Europe's having lost control of this world. The blind spot here is that, in so far as technological globalisation continues, it is also the escalation of the European spirit, for *techno-logos* is European. We see the same blind spot in Henry Kissinger's 2018 article 'How the Enlightenment Ends...', in which Kissinger claims that the Enlightenment spreads its philosophy via technology, and that now, with the global competition in AI, the Enlightenment has come to an end, and a new philosophy is needed. Kissinger here also fails to see that in modern technology are embedded epistemological and onto-logical assumptions that are inseparable from the European spirit; however, he sees clearly that, after the end of the Enlightenment, the West needs a new philosophy of technology.[41] Perhaps Heidegger had the clearest mind of all when he tried to determine the meaning of the end of philosophy in his 1964 article 'The End of Philosophy and the Task of Thinking'. In this article Heidegger proposes that the 'end of philosophy' firstly means its realisation or completion in cybernetics, the most fully actualised principle of *Gestell*, according to which everything is comprehended as feedback loops. Secondly, the end of philosophy is not only ontological but also geopolitical:

40. '[T]he northern slope, Siberia, must be eliminated. This slope, from the Altai chain, with its fine streams, that pour their waters into the northern Ocean, does not at all concern us here; because the Northern Zone, as already stated, lies out of the pale of History.' See G.W.F. Hegel, *Philosophy of History*, tr. J. Sibree (New York: Dover, 1956), 118.

41. H. Kissinger, 'How the Enlightenment Ends', *The Atlantic*, June 2018.

it means, in Heidegger's own words, 'the beginning of the world civilisation based upon Western European thinking'.[42] This second meaning of the end of philosophy, however, has often been overlooked by interpreters of Heidegger. The omnipresence and omnipotence of European technology is a fact that one cannot easily deny; the question yet to be addressed is where this world civilisation is headed and where it might go. For Patočka, Post-Europe is to be seen in the domination of the United States and the American culture—Europe lost in its own planetarism—while, in agreement with Heidegger, I would suggest that we view planetarisation not as the end of Europe, but as the beginning of its planetarisation project.

In the documentary *The Ister*, Stiegler claims audaciously that even Japanese technology is originally Greek: '[A]ll the past is Greek. Even for a Japanese, because technology is Greek.' This remark is an intriguing if not explicit expression of Eurocentrism. From an historical and archaeological point of view, Stiegler must have been aware that Greek technology came largely from the Near East,[43] and that Japan was largely undiscovered by Europeans until the sixteenth century. Why then did he want to claim that the entirety of the past is Greek, even for a Japanese? Doesn't Japan have a past, didn't it have technics? In Stiegler's absence, this puzzle can only be pondered without being definitively resolved. He might have been thinking that Japan abandoned or undermined its own technology and embraced European technology. In which case, is Japan European or Japanese? Did Japan already become European because of its appropriation of European technology? Or is Japan disoriented in this appropriation, becoming neither orient nor occident? Japan did indeed want to become part of Europe.[44] However, through colonisation and globalisation, Europe has already extended everywhere, and has gone beyond being a mere

---

42. M. Heidegger, *On Time and Being*, tr. J. Stambaugh (New York: Harper & Row, 1972), 59.

43. J. Ellul, *The Technological Society* (New York: Vintage, 1964), 27–28.

geographical concept. Today not only Japan, but almost all countries in Asia and Latin America, are becoming Europe. However,
whether this Europeanisation of non-European countries is a desirable future was intensely debated in the twentieth century, and this
debate continues into the twenty-first century.

Stiegler had some contact with Japan through Hidetaka Ishida
in earlier days, and like almost all French philosophers, he was fas-
cinated by the aesthetics of Japan. He went to China for the first
time in 2008, but only had deeper contact with China from 2015 on.
However, Stiegler wasn't particularly interested in Chinese thought
at the outset, since China for him meant Marxism more than anything else. At the same time, he worked a great deal during his stay
in China. He carried two big suitcases of books with him during
his one-month stay and worked all the time in his apartment or in
hotel rooms. It was only at a very late stage that he became more
open to Chinese thought. And it was also in Stiegler's later days
that our conversations become more productive. In the spring of
2019, he told me that he was reading the *Dao de jing* and asked for
recommendations for sinologists' writings on the text. However, all
of this happened too late and in too much of a rush, so he wasn't
able to render his accidental contact with China and the five years of
teaching in two universities there a necessity. In the last two years
before his death, we discussed at length the question of technical
tendency and technical fact, terminologies coined by the palaeon-
tologist and anthropologist André Leroi-Gourhan. However, we
never really confronted one another in the way that both of us
wished to.

---

44. *Datsu-A Ron* (脱亞論), literally 'theory of leaving Asia', is a discourse that
    emerged toward the end of the nineteenth century in Japan, suggesting
    abandoning Qing China and Joseon Korea, and aligning Japan with the
    West. It is often associated with the educator and thinker Yukichi Fukuzawa
    (1835–1901).

§5. INDIVIDUATION and the TASK of THINKING

If we want to talk about Post-Europe or a post-European philosophy today, and if we can speak with Stiegler on this subject, then we might want to connect the question of Spirit with the question of technics. It remains a question for us to reformulate the relation between Post-Europe, philosophy, and technology. European culture and technology are already omnipresent. It is not possible for non-Europeans to de-Europeanise, in the sense of abandoning the technological world; and it is equally impossible for Europe to continue its Eurocentric discourse, because technology is no longer merely European, meaning that the intimate relation between European philosophy and technology is once again becoming contingent.

In the first volume of *Consituer l'Europe* (2005), a rather sketchy work that outlines his reflections on Europe, Stiegler discussed the alarming number of cases of depression in China—according to his data, twenty percent of the Chinese population suffers from depression and of them, one hundred million are deeply depressed. He says that China is becoming capitalist, and, as in the West, whether American or European, 'desire is in grave sufferance'.[45] By this he means that the libidinal economy has become a drive-dominated consumerist economy. In a sense, we can say that he saw already that China and the West are on the same sinking boat of industrial capitalism, that they have all submitted their fate to calculability. This analysis of libidinal economy is at the core of Stiegler's critique of capitalism but also, we might say, of geopolitics. In *For a New Critique of Political Economy*, Stiegler showed how American consumerism became a global paradigm, and how it effectively destroys the libidinal economy by short-circuiting desire and turning this economy into a drive-dominated economy. Stiegler takes the distinction between desire and drive from Freud: desire means investment, for

45. B. Stiegler, *Constituer l'Europe 1 Dans un monde sans vergogne* (Paris: Galilée, 2005), 27.

example, love, friendship, or learning a skill; drive is closer to instinct, for example, when one gets hungry one wants to eat. This distinction between desire and drive allows him to reconstruct a political economy as a new reading of Marx's analysis of proletarianisation. Proletarianisation took place when a shoemaker of the nineteenth century had to leave his workshop and work in the factory which produced similar but standardised shoes. The shoemaker wasn't able to use his own knowledge anymore, but instead repeated the instructions given to him—in other words, he was deskilled. In the consumerist society, proletarianisation takes a more radical turn by short-circuiting the noetic process of learning and therefore the libidinal process of investing, while multiplying phenomena of addiction, for example, shopping, video games, social media, etc. The drive-dominated economy is an economy of disindividuation, meaning that the individual fails to individuate with themselves and with others. In other words, the individual fails to love themselves and therefore also loses the capacity to love others. Precisely in the same book, we read about the task that Stiegler gave to Europe, namely, to conceive a new model of individuation beyond consumerism in the hyperindustrial society:

> [T]he industrial model that breeds this industrial populism must be completely criticised, rethought and reworked: only then will it be possible to build Europe, a Europe that exists as a unity, and a Europe that exists in the minds of Europeans as a future for them and for their fellow human beings on other continents.[46]

46. 'Et cela veut dire que le modèle industriel qui sécrète ce populisme industriel doit être entièrement critiqué, repensé et réélaboré : là seulement est la possibilité de constituer l'Europe, une Europe qui existe comme une unité, et une Europe qui consiste dans les consciences des Européens comme un avenir pour eux et pour leurs congénères des autres continents.' Ibid., 32.

If a post-European philosophy is possible, it will have to confront American consumerism, which is also an individualism *par
excellence*, and propose a different libidinal, cultural, and political economy. This has probably been the fundamental weakness of
Europe since the Second World War: Europe was not able to resist the
market economy and consumerism—the Americanism that Heidegger
described. Therefore, the new model of individuation that Stiegler
calls for will have to overcome individualism as well as the liberal
democracy built upon it. Today we see how individual rights, the
foundation of citizenship, have fallen victim to consumerism and
populism. The market-oriented development of technology empowers
the individual by providing them with tools to develop a seemingly
ever-expanding but closed universe. Modern society is characterised by an atomisation which is further affirmed and reinforced by
the digital infrastructure of social media and personalisation. If we
go back to the theoretical foundation and model of contemporary
social networks, it is not difficult to understand that it is based on
the concept of an atomised society: each individual is considered as
a social atom, and society is an aggregation of the atoms mediated
by social relations. The industrial model of social media reinforces
this individualist model of modern society as well as the individualism intrinsic to it.

This is one of the major problems today regarding the digital society: as Stiegler already pointed out in the first volume of *Technics and
Time*, consumerism, a single standard economic system, dominates
the techno-social system.[47] In other words, consumerism determines
both the development of and interdependence within the technical system and the structuring of the social system. Therefore, the
problem is not only one of rights (for example, the right to choose)
but is more about models of individuation. This doesn't mean that
right is not important. On the contrary, it is fundamental; however, rights can also become merely arbitrary, as Hegel shows in

47. Stiegler, *Technics and Time 1*, 31.

the beginning of his *Outlines of the Philosophy of Right*, without con-
tributing anything to individuation. More than a decade ago, the
inventor of the World Wide Web, Sir Tim Berners-Lee, proposed
a universal right of access to the internet; this is to be admired.
However, this right, if we follow Hegel here, remains abstract and
therefore has the tendency to devolve into arbitrariness instead of
actively striving toward the realm of freedom. Postmodern subjects
are nodes in a network which can be submitted to calculation, as
in graph theory. The concept of mass is no longer only about the
herd, those who blindly believe in advertisement and propaganda.
Instead, with digitisation, especially through the enforced use of
various social media and applications, the mass now also designates
targeted individuals. We live in a transition toward complete digitalisation and individualism. There has been a qualitative change
in the concept of the mass, and therefore also the concept of class.

   If we claimed earlier that Stiegler's analysis of libidinal economy is also intended as a critique of geopolitics, it is because in
this analysis, the United States is not understood as imperialist in
the traditional sense, but rather as the driver of globalisation of
a model of disindividuation that is fundamentally pathological.
Can Europe offer a model of individuation in the hyperindustrial
age, an individuation that is beyond consumerism and beyond
its Eurocentrism? If Habermas and Derrida propose a return to
European sovereignty as autonomous from American imperialism,[48]
Stiegler sees the question of sovereignty more concretely in technology, or more precisely, in the model of individuation to whose
realisation technology is central. In other words, what is at stake
is not having a European Google or Facebook, but rather a new
kind of search engine and social network which could facilitate
individuation. The question that follows is, will this individuation
be beneficial to all souls on the earth? Or will this new model of
individuation be only a demonstration of the superiority of the

48. See footnote 19.

European spirit, namely a return to a certain Eurocentrism because it is again a longing for *Heimat*?[49]

This task is fundamental to a post-European philosophy, because philosophers since the beginning have been physicians of civilisation. Disindividuation implies a profound nihilism in which all values above drives would be considered valueless. The diagnosis of disindividuation demands a prescription for a new model of individuation. However, the prescription must come not only in the form of literature, poetry, or music (although these are all fundamental), but also a new political economy. It is also in this sense that the question of technology is central, as Stiegler claims:

> Were philosophy no longer to be in the world, it would be the death of the world; it would be vile, unworldly [*immonde*]. But this philosophy can only be a political philosophy, that is, a political economy, which is to say a technology as well: an altogether novel relation to technology and society, to the extent that the latter lives essentially through technological questions.[50]

A post-European philosophy is a response to Heidegger's call for the task of thinking, a thinking with and beyond the *Gestell*. 'With' because one can only end in catastrophe if one tries to avoid the danger; 'beyond' because there is a need to go beyond the focus on

---

49. This is another point that Karel Novotný considered to be a risk of Patočka's thinking on Post-Europe, as Novotný writes in 'Europe, Post-Europe, and Eurocentrism': 'According to him, the "open soul" of the Europeans should engender the new world's spiritual attitude. However, if the attitude of the "open soul" is interpreted as the search for the transcendental ground of post-European humanity, there remains an internal risk of Eurocentrism, as the attitude of the spiritual supremacy of Europe would be perpetuated, against which non-European societies subsequently construct a defence and thereby distinguish the new state of affairs' (307).

50. Stiegler, 'The Magic Skin', 109.

efficiency and speed, in order to establish a new politics of technology which is in favour of individuation and against the disindividuation produced by the consumerist society. However, one wonders whether this thinking has to come from Europe alone. Heidegger himself affirmed this by returning to the pre-Socratics; as did Patočka, who proposed to return to the 'care of the soul' in order to invent an 'open soul'. It is possible, and understandable, that Heidegger and Patočka were not exposed to non-European thinking to a degree where they would have felt comfortable to think otherwise. If we want to align ourselves with Patočka, then this open soul has to be not only one that constantly negates its Eurocentrism, but also one that actively individuates with the other. The other may arrive as accident—and according to Aristotle in *Metaphysics*, an accident is close to nothing—however, this accident is also the condition of individuation of thinking; namely, the transformative power of the soul to render what is contingent necessary. (Stiegler didn't talk about the individuation of thinking; the only time we came very close to this subject was during our conference in Taipei in 2019, where I was surprised by Stiegler's lecture on Édouard Glissant and his idea of creolisation.)

What is urgent is not only to invent models of individuation to counter the consumerism that dominates technological innovation today, but also an individuation of thinking. Philosophy has to de-Europeanise itself in this process of individuation. Further, this de-Europeanisation must be interpreted in two ways. Firstly, if what Heidegger says in 'The End of Philosophy and the Task of Thinking' is true, namely that cybernetics marks the end and completion of European philosophy, and if it is true that European philosophy has come to its end, then for philosophy to continue surviving it will have to become post-European. A post-European philosophy should aim for a profound transformative power in regard to technology. It should aim to provide a new theory of individuation which is able to overcome the disindividuation we find in contemporary industrial technology. We will have to transvaluate the concepts of progress, growth, liberty, etc., in order to make space for the development of new models of individuation via technologies. Secondly, this de-Europeanisation should also be understood as an individuation of thinking, as French philosophy was to German philosophy. Maybe we can even say that there is no thinking as such, but only individuation of thinking. This individuation necessarily produces a leap, as a resolution of incompatibilities and tensions. Such individuation of thinking takes place between self and other; this other could be Asia, Africa, Latin America, or even minorities inside Europe itself. But in any case, it means that one has to go beyond comparative philosophy, which remains a subject of the history of philosophy. Instead, one must reactivate a process of *individuation of thinking* in light of technological acceleration.

The pandemic announced the end of the first phase of globalisation after the Cold War: if there is still a common future for the human beings, it will have to become planetary. In the planetary condition, any discourse on the crisis of the European spirit is no longer appropriate—as Derrida reminds us in *The Other Heading*. If there is one element common to Patočka's and Stiegler's visions of a post-European philosophy, it is the question of care, which is expressed as 'care of the soul' in the late Patočka and as *panser/penser* in Stiegler. To address the question of care, however, we will have to pass via a reflection on individuation. As we have tried to suggest above, there are two different directions for talking about individuation: one concerns a new industrial spirit against disindividuation, the other concerns the individuation of thinking beyond the question of essence. We will elaborate upon the latter in the next chapter.

CHAPTER TWO

'WHAT IS ASIA?': A QUESTION

Europe is a concept that does not originate from itself, but from its essential antithesis to Asia.... Europe is originally, and as long as it remains true to itself, politically and spiritually an anti-Asian power.

—Karl Löwith[1]

Inquirer: Here you are touching on a controversial question which I often discussed with Count Kuki—the question whether it is necessary and rightful for Eastasians to chase after the European conceptual systems.

Japanese: In the face of modern technicalization and industrialization of every continent, there would seem to be no escape any longer.

I: You speak cautiously, you say '... would seem ...'

J: Indeed. For the possibility still always remains that, seen from the point of view of our East Asian existence, the technical world which sweeps us along must confine itself to surface matters, and ... that ...

I: ... that for this reason a true encounter with European existence is still not taking place, in spite of all assimilations and intermixtures.

—Martin Heidegger[2]

1. K. Löwith, *Weltgeschichte und Heilsgeschehen: Zur Kritik der Geschichtsphilosophie* (Stuttgart: J.B. Metzlersche, 1983), 475: 'Europa ist ein Begriff, der nicht aus ihn selber stammt, sondern aus seinem wesentlichen Gegensatze zu Asien.... Europa ist ursprünglich, und solang es sich treu bleibt, politisch und geistig eine gegenasiatische Macht.'
2. M. Heidegger, 'A Dialogue on Language', in *On the Way to Language*, tr. P.D. Hertz (New York: Harper & Row, 1971), 3.

§6. The Question 'What Is Asia?'

Is it legitimate to raise the question 'What is Asia?' Is this question possible today? Indeed, was it possible at all in the past?

Let us start by questioning the legitimacy of this ontological question: What is Asia? To ask what Asia is, as one asks what Europe is, we will have to essentialise, asking what makes Asia Asia, as we might ask what makes a tree a tree: namely, we will have to ask after the essence of Asia. In this respect, the question 'What is Asia?' is in itself nothing Asian. It is a European question, not because this question has never been posed in Asia, but because it is a question concerning the being of Asia, an ontological question. Recall here that Kitaro Nishida once claimed that Western philosophy is centred on the question of Being, while Eastern philosophy inquiries into the question of Nothing:

> From a metaphysical standpoint, then, how do we distinguish the forms of culture east and west from one another? I believe we can distinguish the west as having taken being as the ground of reality and the east as having taken nothing as its ground. Or, we might say, the one looked to form, the other to the formless.[3]

If Nishida is correct here, then 'What is Asia?' is either an illegitimate question, or one that may produce a completely unexpected answer. François Jullien, without referring to Nishida, also concluded that there is no ontology in China,[4] and that the identification of ontology with *ben ti lun* (本體論, literally 'theory of the original substance', often translated as 'ontology') is false. This may sound puzzling, since in everyday language one often asks 'What is X?' It is not that non-Europeans have never raised such questions, but

---

3. Heisig, *Philosophers of Nothingness*, 86.

4. F. Jullien, 'Between Is Not Being', *Theory, Culture & Society* 40:4–5 (2023): 239–49.

rather that when they did, these were never inquiries into essence. Essence is that which doesn't change—which is also why substance, as distinguished from accident, was also understood as essence. The inquiry into essence is through *logos*. *Logos* means talking, and also bears other names such as reason, logic, etc. *Logos* comes from *legein*, to lay something in front of. *Logos* means the pursuit of a rationality which is able to reveal the essential by way of ontological inquiries.

To ask 'What is Europe?' is therefore to conduct an inquiry into the essence of Europe. Husserl responded to this question in his 1935 Vienna lecture, in which he states that Europe is not a geographical location, but a spirit. Husserl tries to paint us a *'geistige Gestalt'*, a spiritual figure of Europe, in which the European spirit is described as the infinite task of the pursuit of the universal and the rational:

> 'The spiritual figure of Europe'—what is it? It is exhibiting the philosophical idea immanent in the history of Europe (of spiritual Europe). To put it another way, it is its immanent teleology, which, if we consider mankind in general, manifests itself as a new human epoch emerging and beginning to grow, the epoch of a humanity that from now on will and can live only in the free fashioning of its being and its historical life out of rational ideas and infinite tasks.[5]

The European spirit is its philosophy; if one can talk about an image of such a spirit, it is an immanent teleology in which history is the history of the rational idea. The progress of the rational idea is its search for the universal, and it is only through such an infinite task of searching that new epochs of humanity are made possible. It is difficult, if not impossible, to define Asia in terms of such an image, or in terms of any image at all. Another Kyoto School philosopher,

---

5. E. Husserl, 'Philosophy and the Crisis of European Man', Lecture delivered by Edmund Husserl, Vienna, 10 May 1935, also discussed in chapter 1, above.

Tetsurō Watsuji, gave us rich images of Asia, the Middle East, and Europe in his treatise on *Fûdo*.[6] The term *fûdo* is composed of the two Chinese characters for wind [風] and soil [土], and is often rendered into English as 'climate'; however, *fûdo* is more than climate, since it also means customs and traditions; to some extent, *fûdo* is the formation of culture conditioned by a cosmological and geographical particularity. Asia is heavily affected by monsoons, and according to Watsuji the resulting relative lack of seasonal change creates an easygoing personality—in Southeast Asia especially, since the weather is always very warm, nature provides a plenitude of foodstuffs, and therefore there is no need to labour too much in order to survive, or to worry about the possibility of day-to-day living. Similarly, the lack of natural resources in the deserts of the Middle East creates solidarity between peoples, so that the Jewish people, although they live in diaspora, remain united, while in the meadowlands of Europe, clear and regular seasonal changes demonstrate the constancy of the laws of nature, thus suggesting the possibility of mastering nature with science. In comparison with Husserl's determination of the European spirit, Watsuji didn't give us a typology of ideas, images of spirit, but a topology of tendencies determined by the cosmo-geographical milieu.

Many authors have already pointed out, in retrospect, the Eurocentrism of Husserl's argument on the spiritual image of Europe, in the sense that for him, European humanity seems to mean humanity in general. In comparison with the spiritual unity of Europe, Asia is fragmented; it was not united by a monotheism as Europe was. In mediaeval Europe, despite wars both internal and external and the existence of borders, Christianity nonetheless brought the separated countries together by endowing the individual with an overriding universal and religious identity.[7] Europe was once

6. T. Watsuji, *Climate and Culture: A Philosophical Study*, tr. G. Bownas (Westport, CT: Greenwood Press, 1961).

7. C. Brown, *Sovereignty, Rights and Justice* (Cambridge: Polity, 2002), 20–21.

religiously defined by universal Christian love and philosophically defined by universal rationality; therefore, it was able to claim a spiritual figure, and one that is ontologically universal. In the 1930s Husserl laments the crisis of European science and of the European spirit, now dominated by naturalism and objectivism.[8] He wants to return to the lifeworld, understood as the primary condition of science and of phenomenology as rigorous science. It is beyond us to judge whether phenomenology is capable of saving Europe from its crisis—it was also the deconstructive task of the Derridean school to make such a judgment. What interests us in this context is its generalisation and affirmation of a unified European spirit. In comparison, owing to the lack of monotheism and any discourse of the universal, there has never been any unifying Asian thought. One might find greater similarities among East Asian countries owing to the common adoption of Chinese characters and the early influences of Chinese culture, but when we look at Southeast Asia and Central Asia, these are very different cultural landscapes. A European thinker today can still respond to the question 'What is Europe?' But it is almost impossible for an Asian thinker to ask 'What is Asia?' because Asia includes so many different regions and cultures that one must surely fail in any attempt to generalise *an* Asia.

In the summer of 2022, when I took a taxi to Warsaw Chopin Airport, the driver—a retired lawyer, so he told me—complained about the government, and said to me, 'Poland is as corrupt as Asia'. I didn't understand what he meant, so I remained silent. Because of my silence, he started to explain: 'I didn't mean Asia like Japan and Korea, I mean Kazakhstan and...'. This was a good lesson for me, since this taxi driver had a very different imaginary of Asia from mine. We East Asians often talk about Asia and Asianism, but we imagine that East Asia means Asia, and unconsciously already

8. E. Husserl, *The Crisis of European Sciences and Transcendental Phenomenology: An Introduction to Phenomenological Philosophy*, tr. D. Carr (Evanston, IL: Northwestern University Press, 1970).

exclude central Asian countries. Therefore, with this title 'What is Asia?', while I claim to be speaking about Asia, in fact I myself am only able to speak, *marginally*, about East Asia.

In the context of East Asia, at least, the question of spirit only arrived when nationalism emerged in the face of colonisation. Attempted essentialisations of Chinese thought, Japanese thought, Korean thought, etc. came to the fore as responses to the external challenges. These supposed national modes of thought were reactions to colonisation and modernisation, but mostly to the domination of Western universalism. There were exchanges between different regions, but they were not united by any common identifier. The Japanese project of creating a prosperous circle of East Asia, or a Schmittean *Großraum* (Schmitt's term, adopted by the Kyoto School thinkers during the Second World War) could be seen as an attempt to create a unified Asia. However, one might well ask whether this attempt to unify Asia through industrialisation (in the name of Asianism) was in fact a mimicry of Europe, even though it claimed to be an anti-European movement, since the industrialisation and mechanisation of Europe was, according to these thinkers, one of the sources of its decadence. So we must inquire not only whether the question 'What is Asia?' is legitimate or not as a philosophical inquiry, but also, and probably far more importantly, whether such a 'Europeanisation' (and subsequently Americanisation) is still a desirable future for Asia. If so, then one has to affirm modernisation and even push it to extremes (as is happening now, in fact). If not, are we going to follow an anti-European path? Or, instead, should we ask whether the past and present of Asia could provide other resources for understanding the future, or shed light on the future of the world in the current planetary condition?

It is undeniable that Asia has long been engaged in Europeanising (and then Americanising) itself; as Heidegger's Japanese interlocutor admitted in the mid-twentieth century, 'in the face of modern technicalization and industrialization of every continent, there would seem to be no escape any longer'. In other words, Asians are becoming Europeans no matter how much one would like to deny it.

This can be easily observed not only in political and economic systems, but also in everyday activities such as reading, drinking, eating, and consuming—whereas in Europe, even in some capital cities, all one finds of Asia is a few poor Asian restaurants and a great many esoteric clichés. In his book *Eurotaoism*, Peter Sloterdijk described European modernity as acceleration towards total mobilisation; this mobilisation also produces a fatigue which then demands a Eurotaoism—a quest for some oriental wisdom that can fill the vacuum left behind by the Christian religion after secularisation.[9] This 'Eurotaoism' is of course a satire, but it is also a confirmation of the Heideggerian diagnosis of the occidental illness: Daoism and Buddhism will not help Europe to recover from this fatigue or from this drive to mobilisation. Really, this phenomenon attests only to the ultimate irrelevance of Eastern thinking to the West, while the West continues to mobilise the East with its techno-scientific knowledge and the market economy:

> Even if we recognize Eastern wisdom as an impressive and singular greatness, Asian imports alone will not save the Western-mobilized world. The initiative of 'Americotaoism' is just that—a response to the 'crisis of the West' by importing holistic fast food from the Far East.[10]

But this verdict on the irrelevance of Buddhism and Daoism to the West, just as much as the admission of them as elements of New Age philosophy, excludes these modes of thought from any participation in future world history. And this exclusion might not be all the fault of hippies giving Eastern philosophy a bad name, but could also

9. See P. Sloterdijk, *Infinite Mobilization: Towards a Critique of Political Kinetics*, tr. S. Berjan (Cambridge: Polity, 2020); the original title in German was *Eurotaoismus: Zur Kritik der politischen Kinetik* (Frankfurt am Main: Suhrkamp Verlag, 1989).

10. Sloterdijk, *Infinite Mobilization*, viii.

be owing to the fact that Eastern thought has long been considered inferior by the West, except among specialists of Eastern culture. In the famous symposium 'The Standpoint of World History and Japan' (26 November 1941), Nishitani clearly stated that

> Asia has been for Europeans something to act upon, and it is from that viewpoint alone that they have viewed this part of the world. Europe has acted upon Asia, which has served as the object of its action; not the other way around. It is an 'I' and 'Thou' relationship, and Europe has assumed the role of the 'I': this is its standpoint. But this also explains why the transformation now under way is the stuff of crisis for Europeans, while here it takes the form of a new world order.[11]

For Nishitani, the crisis of Europe is indicated by the breaking down of the I-Thou relation; the Thou is becoming the I, in juxtaposition to the Western I. This I-Thou relation doesn't only exist between the West and the East, but is also internal to the East. That is, the East is also considered inferior by Easterners themselves. At the end of the nineteenth and the beginning of the twentieth century, race and thinking were considered inseparable. The concept of race was not only present, but was also considered to determine the destiny of a people. Before the encounter with Europeans, the Chinese had already made a distinction between *hua* (China, mainly *han* ethnics) and *yi* (barbarians), but such a distinction was not yet based on race or nation. The Sino–barbarian dichotomy [*hua-yi* distinction, 華夷之辨] is dependent on the practice of *li* (rituals, rites), since *li* is at the core of *wen hua* (culture, literally meaning to transform through the teaching of reading and writing), and the *yi* can also be integrated into *hua* by practicing *li* (or being cultivated in the Han's way). The

---

11. D. Williams, *The Philosophy of Japanese Wartime Resistance: A Reading, with Commentary, of the Complete Texts of the Kyoto School Discussions of 'The Standpoint of World History and Japan'* (London: Routledge, 2014), 116.

Ming Confucian Gu Yanwu (顧炎武, 1613–1682) made a distinction between losing the country [亡國] and losing *tianxia* [亡天下]. The former refers only to the change of emperor or dynasty, the latter refers to the destruction of moral order, leading to a situation similar to Hobbes's state of nature.[12] This could be read as an affirmation of the *hua-yi* distinction. But this distinction lost its hold in the nineteenth century, when a theory of race was popularised through the translation of the work of Huxley and Spencer. In China, we can read the implication of this theory of race, for example, in the writings of one of the most important intellectuals, Liu Shipei (劉師培, 1884–1919), considered a great genius:

> When the barbarians invaded China, because Han is a superior race, so China lost the country but not the race; when the Westerners came to the East, in comparison, the Asian race is inferior to the Western race, so one worries not about losing the country [亡國], but more about the extinction of the race [亡種].[13]

Liu considered the Han as a superior race in comparison with the barbarians, so that, even though China was conquered by the Mongolians and the Manchurians, while the country or state is lost, the Chinese race still survives. The Westerners, however, are no barbarians. Indeed, in comparison with Westerners, the Asians are an inferior race. Liu therefore feared for the extinction of the Asian race because, according to the Darwinian theory of evolution

---

12. Gu Yanwu, *Ri Zhi Lu* (《日知錄》), chapter 13: 「有亡國, 有亡天下, 亡國與亡天下奚辨? 曰: 易姓改號謂之亡國。仁義充塞, 而至於率獸食人, 人將相食, 謂之亡天下。」, <https://ctext.org/wiki.pl?if=gb&chapter=614214>.

13. Cited by Yuzo Mizoguchi (溝口雄三), *China as Method* (Taipei: National Institute for Compilation and Translation, 1999), 51; from 《劉申叔先生遺書》卷一, 「中國, 當蠻族入主時, 蠻族劣而漢族優, 故雖有亡國而無亡種; 當西人東漸後, 亞種劣而歐種優, 故憂亡國、更憂亡種。」

popularised during Liu's time, the Chinese as a race would become
obsolete or disappear. Following this logic, one might arrive at the
conclusion that Chinese thought couldn't compete with Western
thought, since the former is the product of an inferior race. Of course,
Liu was not the only person who espoused a race-based political
thinking; it was a dominant theory at the time. Kang Youwei (康有
為, 1858–1927), a reformist and one of the most prominent intellectuals of the late Ching dynasty, in his *Datong shu* (大同書, *The Book of
Great Unity*) also declared that the white race was superior, followed
by the yellow, and lastly the brown and black. In order to achieve
the great unity, then, it was necessary to eliminate the difference of
races by turning everyone into whites. According to him, if the yellow race were to change their diet to medium rare beef steak and
immigrate from the warm south to the cold north then, after two or
three generations, they would turn into whites.[14] Although it seemed
to him an insuperable problem, he nevertheless also proposed ways
to turn the black into white, which we shall not detail here. This theory of race, coming from one of the most important intellectuals and
reformists of the late Ching dynasty, seems laughable today, but it
shows that biopolitics has always been in play since the beginning
of colonisation.

In the eyes of the Kyoto School thinkers, at least those who participated in the symposiums of 1941 and 1942, China became the
'Thou' and Japan the 'I'. They argued that China's subordination
to Western civilisation was able to take place because China had
long considered itself the centre of the world and as superior to
other Asian countries; when it encountered Western civilisation

---

14. Kang Youwei (康有為), *The Book of Great Unity* (《大同書》), 「凡日食用煎牛肉半
生熟、血尚紅滴者，行之數月，面即如塗脂矣。若多行太陽之中，挹受日光，游居通
風之地，吸受空氣，加以二三代合種之傳，稍移南人於北地，更易山人於江濱，不過
百年，黃種之人，皆漸為白色，加以通種，自能合化，故不待大同之成，黃人已盡為
白人矣。是二種者已合為一色，無自辨別，惟棕、黑二種與白人遠絕，真難為合者也。」
<https://ctext.org/wiki.pl?if=gb&chapter=547649>.

with its more advanced science and technology, China promptly abandoned its sense of superiority. The result, as Suzuki concludes, was 'a new kind of Europeanized Chinese'. Japan, on the contrary, exhibited a very different psychology in its encounter with Western civilisation.[15] Japan didn't subordinate itself to the West. Instead its *moralische Energie* (in Leopold von Ranke's sense) grew, and with its self-consciousness of its role in world history, Japan became the leader of Asia as well as the world. Nishitani recalled how, during his trip to Germany, he passed by Shanghai, and a Filipino sailor told him how much he admired Japan and he wished that one day the Philippines would follow its lead. Commenting on the Filipino sailor's wish, Nishitani claims:

> Over the course of its long history, Japan has fostered a [sober and disciplined] culture, and therefore we have completed the apprenticeship of civilization. In other words, well before the arrival of European civilization on these shores, Japan could boast a highly developed culture, one animated by an affective life force. The Philippines lacks such foundations. Therefore, even if the Philippines absorbed the products of European civilization on a Japanese scale, the result would be very different.[16]

In the transcripts of the symposiums, we can read many more comments on Japan's superiority in comparison to the Chinese, Koreans, Indonesians, etc. This superiority comes first of all out of a belief in *Blut und Boden* (when Nishitani read in a book that Indonesians are aristocrats, he added that he had heard that the Indonesians have Japanese blood...), and secondly from a historical self-consciousness on the part of Japan—a people is able to feel that they are creating a new world order, writing world history.

15. Williams, *The Philosophy of Japanese Wartime Resistance*, 199.
16. Ibid., 202.

In the twentieth century, postcolonialism attempted to destroy the hierarchy of cultures, namely the superiority of Western culture and the inferiority of non-Western culture, which was also defined according to the degree of paleness of the skin. More than a hundred years after Liu Shipei and Kang Youwei, racial politics became politically incorrect in mainstream discourse, although it continued to exist in people's minds. Today, Asian thought is becoming more respected in terms of historical and comparative studies. However, its relevance to contemporary society is still not seen as significant. One of the key reasons for this is that Asian thought is apparently unable to engage with contemporary technological society: apart perhaps from being able to provide an ethics of technology, be it Buddhist, Daoist or Confucian, it no longer speaks to the world of today. It is for this reason we must look into the question concerning technology.

§7. Technology and the Limit of Comparative Studies

The Europeanisation and Americanisation of Asia is undoubtedly underway, something that was evident in Husserl's 'Crisis of European Science', where he speaks of the 'Europeanisation of other peoples [*Europäisierung aller fremden Menschheiten*]'. Our question is: Can Asia contribute a different perspective on the becoming of the world? Can Asian thought contribute to contemporary thought? We can only speak in the future tense here: Asian thought without doubt harbours important resources for thinking, but their relevance to contemporary society is yet to be ascertained. This doesn't mean that they have no role to play in the present. It is undeniable that Asian modes of thinking, no matter how implicitly, play a significant role in everyday life in Asian communities, as an unconscious that intervenes in the formation of tastes, gestures, and values. However, in the landscape of contemporary thought, their contribution has yet to be elaborated and developed.

Between the late nineteenth century and early twentieth century, the West was considered to be a more advanced culture, and Europe meant the 'world'. However, as the Japanese historian and sinologist Yuzo Mizoguchi (溝口雄三, 1932–2010) argued in his famous *China as Method* (方法としての中国), once we give up using the 'world' (i.e., the 'European world') to measure China, and recognise the world as a diversity and China as a singular element of this world alongside Europe, then we can rediscover a *noodiversity*. Mizoguchi was partially responding here to research on China in Japan, which still placed China on a timeline defined by the West, on which China was inevitably revealed to be backward and behind. For Mizoguchi, concepts such as 'freedom', 'state', 'law', and 'contract' could be understood in ways other than how they are defined in European thought, and the world would then appear to us as a diversity instead of a homogeneity within which one can compare the advancement of different nations.[17] Writing in 1989, Mizoguchi believed that using Europe as a monistic standard for Asia was already an obsolete approach.[18] One cannot help but relate this to Nishitani's claims regarding the peripherality of Europe before the Second World War, and Patočka's concept of Post-Europe after the Second World War. According to both of them, Europe ceased to be a world power—in other words, Europe lost the privilege of being the dominant force of the world civilisation. This reopening of the world as diversity or pluralism already signifies the end of European domination. This noodiversity implies a diversity of intellectual histories, concepts and ideas.

However, I think that this idea of a liberation from the domination of Europe might be only an illusion, albeit one motivated by goodwill. We find this illusion—but in a rather intriguing way—in Yoshimi Takeuchi's 'Asia as Method', a precursor to Mizoguchi's *China as Method*. Takeuchi, like Mizoguchi, was also a China scholar. He compared modernisation in China with modernisation in Japan following John Dewey's observations and his own experience. Takeuchi claims that modernisation in Japan takes place largely from outside, and

17. Mizoguchi, *China as Method*, 105–7.
18. Ibid., 109.

therefore that it is superficial and will fall apart, while modernisation in China is internally generated.[19] The evidence he gives to support his claim that modernisation in China arose internally is the protests during the May Fourth movement in 1919. It so happened that during this time, both John Dewey and Bertrand Russell were in China, and both of them also compared Japan with China. During the protests, the Chinese students knew that they might be arrested, but they still took to the streets. In other words, for Takeuchi, the craving for democracy in China was not caused by external forces, but rather emerged from a self-awareness and self-affirmation among the Chinese students. Takeuchi's encounter with the writings of Lu Xun (鲁迅, 1881–1936) confirmed his observation, and supported his view that modernisation in China was grounded in its 'ethnic-national characteristics'.[20] However, isn't Europe still the standard of reference here, since modernisation and its related mode of individuation is still considered as the standard of comparison among Asian countries and as the ultimate aim of the nation?[21] For Takeuchi, paradoxically, modernisation also means resistance against colonial power, in the sense that the East has to catch up in order not to be defeated.[22] Therefore there is no real dichotomy between the East and the West, but rather a Hegelian dialectics. This is revealed in the intriguing conclusion of 'Asia as Method':

19. Y. Takeuchi, 'Asia as Method', in *What Is Modernity?*, ed., tr. Calichman (New York: Columbia University Press, 2005), 156.

20. Ibid., 164.

21. There is unfortunately a lack of distinction between modernisation and modernity in Takeuchi's writing. In 'What Is Modernity? (the Case of Japan and China)', Takeuchi gives a definition of modernity which is fundamentally Hegelian: 'the self-recognition of Europe as seen within history, that regarding of itself as distinct from the feudalistic, which Europe gained in the process of liberating itself from the feudal (a process that involved the emergence of free capital in the realm of production and the formation of personality qua autonomous and equal individuals with respect to human beings)' (54).

Rather the Orient must re-embrace the West, it must change the West itself in order to realize the latter's outstanding cultural values on a greater scale. Such a rollback of culture or values would create universality. The Orient must change the West in order to further elevate those universal values that the West itself produced. This is the main problem facing East-West relations today, and it is at once a political and cultural issue.[23]

How could the East elevate the West toward true universality? Is this done in order to produce a universal more modern than the West? This might be what Takeuchi means, but he often seems to be confused by the 'dual structures' he himself created.[24]

The decline of the West had already been announced by Paul Valéry, Oswald Spengler, and many others. In his short 1931 book *Man and Technics*, Spengler argued that the West was making a huge mistake by exporting its technology:

[A]t the close of last century, the blind will-to-power began to make its decisive mistakes. Instead of keeping strictly to itself the technical knowledge that constituted their greatest asset, the 'white' peoples complacently offered it to all the world, in every Hochschule, verbally and on paper, and the astonished homage of Indians and Japanese delighted them.[25]

22. 'The history of resistance is the history of modernization, and there is no modernization that does not pass through resistance.' Takeuchi, 'What Is Modernity?', 57.

23. Takeuchi, 'Asia as Method', 165.

24. Above, we discussed his 'dual structure of the Greater East Asia War', namely that Japan's war in Asia is a decolonial project at the same time as an imperial project.

25. O. Spengler, *Man and Technics: A Contribution to a Philosophy of Life*, tr. C.F. Atkinson (London: Allen & Unwin, 1932), 100–101.

As a result, continues Spengler, the Japanese became 'technicians of the first rank, and in their [1904–5] war against Russia they revealed a technical superiority from which their teachers were able to learn many lessons'.[26] Japan exposed the dilemma of technological globalisation: on one hand, the spread of technology constructs a global axis of time through which European modernity becomes the synchronising metric of all civilisations; on the other, the same spread frees modern science and technology from being the exclusive asset of European modernity, rendering the West vulnerable to global competition. This apparent decline [*Untergang*] confirmed what Patočka and Mizoguchi were claiming. However, undoubtedly the story is not this simple.

Perhaps we can contrast this claim with what Martin Heidegger says in his 1964 'The End of Philosophy and the Task of Thinking'. Heidegger claims here that 'The end of philosophy means: the beginning of the world civilization based upon Western European thinking.'[27] What Heidegger means is that cybernetics is the fulfilment or realisation of Western metaphysics, and that this technological world will be the foundation of the world civilisation; therefore, even though it looks as if the world is liberated from Europe, in fact the world-civilisation will inevitably build upon European metaphysics (now in the form of technology). We might say that Heidegger was cynical, nevertheless he was not wrong. Therefore, turning to *China as Method* or *Asia as Method*[28] gives us a different intellectual history or histories, which without doubt are important for understanding the history of thought and how it was repressed by colonialism; they also affirm a pluralism which is what makes the world (no longer in a European sense) possible. However,

26. Ibid.

27. M. Heidegger, 'The End of Philosophy and the Task of Thinking', in *On Time and Being*, tr. J. Stambaugh (Chicago: University of Chicago Press, 2002), 59.

28. See also K.H. Chen, *Asia as Method: Toward Deimperialization* (Durham, NC: Duke University Press, 2010).

this affirmation of diversity is only the first step; that is to say, it is not yet sufficient to respond to this new condition of technological planetarisation, otherwise it would quickly become nothing more than the introduction of a cultural relativism.

I have no intention of undermining the significance of Takeuchi, Mizoguchi, and other scholars who have been on the same front fighting against Western hegemony, indeed I have a great deal of respect for intellectual historians and postcolonialist scholars who give us different landscapes of thought than those we had become accustomed to taking for granted. I just want to suggest that we have to go further by tackling the question of technology, which has been conceptually underestimated during modernisation in Asia. In general, during the process of modernisation, technology is considered merely an instrument. We may recall how, during modernisation in the second half of the nineteenth century, East Asian countries thought that they could master Western technologies using their own thought. The British historian Arnold Toynbee raised an interesting question in his 1952 Reith Lectures for the BBC: Why did the Chinese and Japanese refuse European visitors in the sixteenth century, but allow them to enter their countries in the nineteenth century? His answer was that in the sixteenth century the Europeans wanted to export both religion and technology to East Asia, and Asians realised that that would mean a change in their form of life. Toward the end of the seventeenth century, according to Toynbee, something happened in Europe: technology and religion became separated (this is a passage heavily commented on and criticised by Carl Schmitt).[29] In the nineteenth century, the Europeans understood that it was more effective to just export technology without Christianity. And the Asian countries easily accepted that technology was something inessential and instrumental, that they were 'users' who could decide how to use them. Toynbee continues as follows:

29. See C. Schmitt, 'Die Einheit der Welt', in *Staat, Großraum, Nomos Arbeiten aus den Jahren 1916–1969* (Berlin: Duncker und Humblot, 1995), 496–512.

Technology operates on the surface of life, and therefore it
seems practicable to adopt a foreign technology without putting oneself in danger of ceasing to be able to call one's soul
one's own. This notion that, in adopting a foreign technology,
one is incurring only a limited liability may, of course, be a
miscalculation.[30]

What Toynbee was saying is that technology in itself is nothing
neutral; it carries particular forms of knowledge and practice, with
which it obliges its users to comply. If one does not take this into
consideration, one is liable to adopt a rather dualist approach,
undermining the importance of technology by treating it as merely
something instrumental. In Asia during this period, we find very
similar slogans such as 'Chinese substance and Western function
[中體西用]', 'Japanese soul and Western knowledge [和魂洋才]', or
'Eastern Dao and Western Qi [동도서기론]'. All of these movements
share the conviction that Eastern thinking will be able to master
Western science and technology, which are mere instruments. Today,
those familiar with the criticism of dualism and modernity know
that this wishful thinking is only a variation of Cartesian dualism,
and it is doomed to fail since it was a product of early modernity.
However, this stereotype is still prevalent in Asia, for industrialism is
separated from traditional thought, except where the latter is mobil-
ised as compensation for the catastrophe caused by the former. The
problem is, however, that if we continue to undermine technology
by seeing it as an instrument to be mastered by Asian thinking, or
if we simply see it as inferior to any intellectual discourse, we are
not far away from the attitudes of the late nineteenth century, and a
modernity which we thought had been overcome will go on and on.

A similar observation and testimony is to be found in the writings of Karl Löwith, an exile in Japan from 1936 to 1941. In his

30. A. Toynbee, *The World and the West* (Oxford: Oxford University Press, 1953), 67.

'Afterword to Japanese Readers', an appendix to the Japanese translation of the long essay *European Nihilism*,[31] Löwith commented on the problem of modernisation in Japan and the need for Japan to confront its naive adoption of Western science and technology, while also lamenting that such awareness would already come 'too late':

> In the latter half of the nineteenth century, when Japan began to make contact with Europe, it took in European 'progress' with admirable energy and zealous speed. European culture, however, while it had advanced and conquered the entire world on the surface, had itself actually decayed internally. But, unlike the Russians in the nineteenth century, the Japanese at that time did not confront Europe in a critical manner. And what the leading figures of Europe from Baudelaire to Nietzsche saw through and sensed a crisis in, the Japanese at the beginning adopted tout court, naively and uncritically. And when they came to know the Europeans better it was already too late; the Europeans had already lost faith in their own civilization. Moreover, the Japanese never paid any attention to self-criticism—which is the best thing about the Europeans.[32]

This appendix to Löwith's book is arguably more interesting than the rest of its ramblings from Hegel to Nietzsche via Flaubert, Baudelaire, Dostoyevsky, and Tolstoy. Löwith claims that in Europe there is a

31. K. Löwith, 'Nachwort an den japanischen Leser', in *Sämtliche Schriften 2 Weltgeschichte und Heilsgeschehen*, 532–40. 'Afterword to Japanese Readers' (日本の読者に与える跋), in *European Nihilism* (ヨーロッパのニヒリズム), tr. Jisaburō Shibata (Tokyo: Chikuma Shobō, 1948).

32. Cited in K. Nishitani, *The Self-Overcoming of Nihilism*, tr. G. Parkes with Setsuko Aihara (New York: SUNY Press, 1990), 176; from K. Löwith, 'Der europäische Nihilismus. Betrachtungen zur Vorgeschichte des europäischen Krieges', in *Weltgeschichte und Heilsgeschehen: Zur Kritik der Geschichtsphilosophie*, 533–34.

culture of self-criticism. Self-criticism, according to Löwith, sets out from a polar opposition, and finally achieves reconciliation. However, he observes that in Japan, the opposition between East and West was not taken seriously. This claim comes out of one of his observations of his Japanese students' attitude towards the West and the East. What Löwith saw was a confusing parallelism between two modes of thought that did not really make contact: Japanese students studied Western philosophy without relating those concepts such as 'will', 'freedom', and 'spirit' to Japanese thought, as if what they were learning was self-evident.[33] Löwith was amazed that his students at the university in Sendai were able to read Hegel in German, Plato in Greek, Hume in English, the Old Testament in Hebrew, and that his assistant was able to read mediaeval German literature in its original language, which even Löwith himself didn't understand. However, he lamented that 'all these books were merely books for them, unrelated to their proper historical background and unrelated to the Japanese feeling and thinking'.[34] Löwith characterised this tendency in Japanese culture as a 'unity without opposition [*gegensatzlose Einheit*]'.[35] Whether this observation is accurate or not is a question I have attempted to analyse in *Art and Cosmotechnics*, therefore we will not elaborate upon it here.[36] However, the phenomenon he

33. Löwith, 'Der europäische Nihilismus', 537.
34. K. Löwith, 'Japanese Westernization and Moral Foundation', 546. It is interesting to note that the late Löwith seemed to have changed his attitude when he compared Japan with America. In Japan, he was able to teach in German as a European philosophy, but in America, he could not be a European anymore. This separation that he found problematic in Japan seems to be a countermodel to America, and in this sense, Japan allows an old Europe to co-exist within its own culture. I am grateful to professor Tanehisa Otabe for sharing this observation with me, which he presented in an unpublished paper with the title 'Karl Löwith and Japanese Thinking That Consists of Two Floors: A Contribution to Intercultural Aesthetics' (2010).
35. Löwith, 'Der europäische Nihilismus', 538n9.

observed, namely the mutual irrelevance of Western knowledge and Eastern thinking, remains a problem today. As we saw in the introduction above, Nishitani found it necessary to respond to Löwith's formulation: '[W]hat [Löwith] says is true [...]. As a European, Löwith let the question lie there. It is our problem, a problem of will.'[37] For Nishitani, the problem is even more serious than Löwith's description implies. Because there is a continuity in the West from Greek philosophy to Christian theology and then to modern science and technology, even when science and technology become determinative, other traditions can still actively participate in it. However, Nishitani states,

> For us in Japan, things are different. In the past, Buddhism and Confucian thought constituted such a basis, but they have already lost their power, leaving a total void and vacuum in our spiritual ground. Our age probably represents the first time since the beginning of Japanese history that such a phenomenon has occurred.[38]

The 'total void' here is alarming, since it implies a complete disorientation. Nishitani's response was logically sound and probably cannot be improved upon: 'the point is to recover the creativity that mediates the past to the future and the future to the past (*but not to restore a bygone era*)'.[39] This resonates of course with Heidegger's approach of returning to the Greeks without restoring a Greek epoch, as well as with Masao Maruyama's proposal to reactivate the *kosō* (古層, literally 'ancient layer') from the present.[40] However, as we have tried to show already in *The Question Concerning Technology in China*,

36. See Y. Hui, *Art and Cosmotechnics* (New York and Minneapolis: e-flux/ University of Minnesota Press, 2021).
37. Nishitani, *The Self-Overcoming of Nihilism*, 176.
38. Ibid., 175.
39. Ibid., 179.

Nishitani's rejection of modern science and technology is largely responsible for the failure of his project of overcoming modernity.

A response proper to our epoch seems to necessarily proceed in two important directions. Firstly, concerning the relevance of Asian thought to the technological epoch in which we are living, I feel that the obsolescence or absence of Asian thought in the landscape of contemporary thought owes to the fact that it failed to address the question of technology beyond a classical humanism which emphasises the value of human morality and responsibility. This humanism might have functioned well in certain socio-economical settings when technologies were limited to simple tools, but once the technological condition radically changed, for example with a high degree of automation of machines and a large technological system, it might cease to produce the same effect within society. Since Asian thought set itself against technology in an opposition between tradition and modernity, it has been slowly retreating to the status of new age therapy as antidote to the burnout society, even in Asia. We therefore have a techno-scientific modernisation in parallel with a preservation of tradition or traditional thought. The separate existence of the two in parallel cannot last long, though, since it only presents a melancholia which will finally be left behind by rapid technological transformation; everything of the past comes to take the form of nostalgic cultural commodities, i.e., memories become souvenirs. Therefore, this parallelism has to be rethought, and for traditions to have value other than as projects of preservation, it is imperative that Asian thought is rethought or even reconstructed from the perspective of technology, otherwise it will always fail to address contemporary society; and if the debate today continues to be dominated by 'authentic' interpretations

---

40. See M. Maruyama (丸山眞男), 'The Kosō of Historical Consciousness' (「「歴 史意識」の古層」), in *Collected Work of Masao Maruyama Vol. 10* (『丸山眞男集 第10巻』) (Tokyo: Iwanami, 2003), where Maruyama starts with a rereading of the myths in the *Kojiki* (古事記, 'Records of Ancient Matters') in order to demonstrate the *kosō* as a force which is always at work throughout history.

of Asian thought (although these are not without historical importance), it can only fail. In his earlier work, Bernard Stiegler attempted
to reconstruct European philosophy from the perspective of technology, and proposed technology as first philosophy. The reconstruction
of Asian thought has to set out in a similar but differently nuanced
way: it is not a question of comparative philosophy, but rather of
reading the history of philosophy and exposing its limits from the
perspective of technology.

This is only the first step, however, because such a project cannot
avoid the essentialising tendency, and therefore risks falling back
into an ethnocentrism, or even worse, a tribalism. This brings us to
the second direction, or second step, which concerns what I call the
individuation of thinking. This second direction is closely linked to
the first, and we will explain why below, but for now let us explore
the meaning of the individuation of thinking.

As mentioned in the previous chapter, we take the concept of
individuation from Gilbert Simondon. For Simondon, individuation
explains how an individual comes to be an individual. Simondon
critiqued traditional theories of individuation in Western classical
philosophy, namely hylomorphism and atomism: since hylomorphism already presupposes the individuated form, it is something
to be explained by individuation rather than an explanation of it;
as for atomism, it is rejected on the grounds that it relies on mere
chance events, and fails to explain the necessity of individuation.
The critique of hylomorphism also rejects the promotion of form
[eidos] as essence [ousia], because, according to Simondon, it is gen-
esis rather than form that accounts for the individuality of a being,
a thinking, or a culture. By the same token, the essentialisation of
culture does not facilitate the individuation of thinking, but only
reinforces a reluctance to change.

According to Simondon, individuation presupposes a system full
of incompatibility and tensions; when a certain threshold is reached,
the system begins to destructuralise and restructuralise, before reach-
ing a metastability. Simondon frequently employed the example of
crystallisation to demonstrate the process of individuation. Consider

a supersaturated solution of sodium chloride (salt) in which tension between the positive and negative ions arrives at a threshold. Now, when a small amount of energy is applied, the solution starts forming crystals as a way to resolve the tensions, while at the same time heat is released and triggers crystallisation in other regions of the solution. This crystallisation will stop when the system arrives at a metastable state, namely when it becomes relatively stable but not at equilibrium (absolute stability). Crystallisation is only a primitive example of the individuation of physical beings, and it is far from being able to fully account for the individuation of a living being or a psychical being. Nevertheless, it represents a paradigm of individuation in which relations and system, rather than substance and form, are the determining factors in the process. A system sets boundaries so that one can isolate the analysis of relations included in the system. Individuation presupposes tension or, more precisely, incompatibility in the system. Individuation means the discovery of incompatibilities and the resolution of them in order to arrive at a metastable state. We hesitate to call it dialectical, because individuation is not necessarily dialectical—on the contrary, dialectics is a form of individuation.

Simondon's example provides us with some key elements to understand what we call the individuation of thinking here. By elaborating on the individuation of thinking, we also wish to extend his theory of individuation, which, in his *Individuation in Light of Notions of Form and Information*, he limits to the levels of the physical being (crystallography), living being (modern biology) and psychical being (Jungian psychology).[41] If we look for an incompatibility (therefore also differences) between Asian thought and European thought (and this is not limited to only Asia and Europe) against the backdrop of our own epoch, it is not that we want to essentialise Europe or Asia, but rather that we want to identify a condition in which an individuation of thinking could become possible.

---

41. See G. Simondon, *Individuation in Light of Notions of Form and Information*, tr. T. Adkins (Minneapolis: University of Minnesota Press, 2020).

§8. Individuation of Thinking and the Pursuit of the Universal

In the conversation between Heidegger ('the Inquirer') and the Japanese guest quoted in the epigraph of this chapter, we can hear the embarrassment of the Japanese guest: Asia has been imitating Europe in terms of technological and economic development, but a profound dialogue, a 'true encounter with European existence', is still missing. A true dialogue is not only about communication but rather individuation—therefore it is less a question of what is called *thinking*, and more of the *individuation of thinking*.

I want to make a distinction here between individuation and cross-breeding or *métissage*, or what Édouard Glissant calls creolisation. Creolisation normally means that elements of different cultures are blended together to create a new culture, but for Glissant it means something more. Creolisation is like a rhizome that creates multiple roots. For Glissant, creolisation is a diversification, 'one of the poetic dreams of the expanding West', but at the same time an 'antidote to the universal empire that this expansion subsumed'.[42] This diversification through language, literature, and technology is essential for our imagination of a world to come: Glissant asks 'How is it possible to come out of seclusion if only two or three languages continue to monopolize the irrefutable powers of technology and their manipulation, which are imposed as the sole path to salvation and energized by their actual effects?'[43] To give a concrete example, during the colonisation of Hong Kong, the locals invented a drink called *yuenyeung* (literally mandarin duck), which is a mixture of milk tea (a strong black tea with condensed milk) and coffee. Therefore, this kind of *métissage* might be important for one's everyday life once it develops into a habit, and it might stand as an identity of a community, but

---

42. E. Glissant, 'Creolization in the Making of the Americas', *Caribbean Quarterly* 54:1–2 (2008): 82.

43. E. Glissant, *Poetics of Relation*, tr. B. Wing (Ann Arbor: University of Michigan Press, 1997), 108.

it doesn't take thinking further. On the contrary, thinking is not a patchwork: it actualises itself not through collage, but by individuating itself. I am doubtful whether creolisation is equivalent to what we call individuation of thinking here, although they could both be seen as efforts to diversify. If creolisation could be understood as a historical process, maybe the individuation of thinking could be understood as an analytic model, and may give us some hints about future strategies.

We should say a few words here also on the difference between the individuation of thinking and what Peter Sloterdijk called Eurotaoism, 'holistic fast food' or 'tender aquarian chop-suey'. Sloterdijk went to the ashram of the Indian new age guru Godman Rajneesh in 1979 and stayed there for four months. In an interview with the *Suddeutsche Zeitung*, Sloterdijk recalls:

> Something I once called the eastward expansion of reason began. With this impulse came a profound uplifting of my being. I was suddenly freed from the psychosocial depression that had hung over my life and that of my generation.[44]

Ten years later (*Eurotaoism* was published in 1989) Sloterdijk realised that this uplifting experience of the relief of his psychosocial depression was synonymous with the West's Asiamania or its desire for a renaissance of antiquity, even if that antiquity is no longer Western but rather comes in a foreign form.[45] Retrospectively, this Asiamania was also a byproduct of globalisation, as exhausted young

---

44. P. Sloterdijk and S. Michaelsen, 'Man denkt an mich, also bin ich' (2014), <https://sz-magazin.sueddeutsche.de/wissen man-denkt-an-mich-also-bin-ich-80778>.

45. 'If a logic of the Renaissance really exists, then the new Asiamania should be read as a sign that creative members of the post-Christian civilization hope to come to an understanding of themselves by grasping at antiquity once again—but this time not so that it can be appropriated as one's *own* antiquity, but as antiquity in a foreign form.' Sloterdijk, *Infinite Mobilization*, 26.

American and European expats had the privilege of meeting their spiritual guru and enjoying the exoticness of Asia. It is the mise-en-scène of a Hegelian comedy in which, by travelling to the East, European *Geist* recognises its own provenance; however, now the Eastern world is transformed into a replica of the Western world, and the 'eastward expansion of reason' is seen as the beginning of an unhappy consciousness.

Apparently, Sloterdijk's observation that apocalypticism has already triumphed as the goal of the world history has been proved right.[46] However, the task of thinking is still far from being elaborated. Heidegger's return to the presocratics in his quest for the thinking of Being is still a pursuit of a European essence against its post-European destiny. The individuation of thinking, which we set up as a task of a post-European philosophy, has to spread its wings before the dusk falls. I want to give two examples of how the individuation of thinking could be understood, and I hope with these two examples to be able to clarify the opportunity and how it could help us to think about the future, if we still believe in philosophy. I will take Mou Zongsan (1909–1995) and Kitaro Nishida (1870–1945), two representative figures of twentieth-century East Asian thinking, as examples with which to sketch a *method* that was followed in practice, without being explicitly elaborated.

Mou Zongsan performed an individuation of Chinese thinking through and with Kantianism, which for him stood as the culmination of Western thinking. Mou set out by creating an incompatibility between Chinese thought and Western thought through his reading of Kant's distinction between phenomenon and noumenon. Kant limits scientific knowledge to phenomena, since human beings only

---

46. 'The warning disaster is itself supposed to be the disaster warning. The actually occurring transformation into light is supposed to critically examine our civilizational process. Those who follow this logic to its conclusion will arrive at a fatal conclusion: only an apocalypse could act as a convincing warning against an apocalypse.' Ibid., 41.

have sensible intuition and therefore can only experience phenomena. This is also the limit of scientific knowledge, beyond which there are only postulates and speculations which may fall prey to *Schwärmerei*, overenthusiasm or fanaticism. Opposed to the phenomenon is the noumenon, which can only be grasped via an intellectual intuition, something which is absent in human beings, and present only in God. In the first edition of the *Critique of Pure Reason*, noumenon also bears the name thing-in-itself. Mou Zongsan claimed that if the strength of Western thought lies in its theorisation of phenomena, which gives rise to science and technology, the strength of Eastern thought lies in its pursuit of the noumenon (where the noumenal entities are not treated as postulates). Now, Chinese thought and Western thought are opposed via this reading of Kant. We find here an incompatibility that is not immediately resolved: Chinese thought cannot be reduced to Western thought, and vice versa. With his reading, Mou Zongsan wants to overcome this incompatibility, but also seeks to show that it is possible to give a new framework to Chinese thought, so that it can also accommodate the possibility of modern science and technology. This leads to Mou Zongsan's reinterpretation of the dictum 'one heart opens two doors' from the *Awakening of Faith in the Mahayana* [大乘起信論]. That is to say, Chinese thought, even though it is centred on the understanding of the noumenon, is able to produce a theory of knowledge based on the phenomenon through a self-negation [自我坎陷]. Mou Zongsan's interpretation of Kant and especially the nou-menon is not uncontroversial,[47] but for us his philosophical method is more important than the defects of his interpretation.

Chinese historians of philosophy are sceptical of Mou's writing since, according to them, Mou distorted Chinese thought by Westernising it, and therefore Mou's elaboration of Chinese thought is far from being authentic, and may even be completely misleading. This criticism is rather tragic, since it fails to understand that Mou was actually looking for a different framework within which an individuation of thinking could take place. If Chinese philosophers limit themselves

47. See *The Question Concerning Technology in China*, §18.

to Chinese thought and dedicate themselves solely to the elaboration of the uniqueness of Chinese thought, an individuation of thinking will not take place; instead, we will only be reminded again and again of the absolute difference between self and other. It is probably not uncommon to find in the East experts in this or that Western philosopher, but it is rare to find an original thinker. Recall that above, we saw how Löwith (1943) lamented that his Japanese students were not able to relate their studies of Western philosophy to their own tradition, and according to him, in the Japan of that time there was only one original thinker: Kitaro Nishida, whose methodology, however, remained still an adaption of the Western one.[48]

Nishida began by asserting that the central question in Western philosophy is Being and that in Eastern philosophy it is Nothing (Nishida was inspired by Zen Buddhism, as he had set himself the task of producing a communication between Zen and philosophy). It is debatable whether this categorisation can be justified or not. However, for Nishida, Eastern thought and Western thought have different beginnings, namely Being and Nothing, and this opposition also implies an incompatibility between Western and Eastern

48. 'The Japanese have today only one original thinker, Nishida, who is comparable to any of the living philosophers of the West in depth of thought and subtlety[....] But even this man's work is no more than an adaptation of Western methodology, the use of it for a logical clarification of the fundamental Japanese intuitions about the world. He attempts to understand in terms of Western philosophy the Buddhist experience and notion of "nothingness".' Löwith, 'The Japanese Mind: A Picture of the Mentality that We Must Understand if We are to Conquer', in *Weltgeschichte und Heilsgeschehen: Zur Kritik der Geschichtsphilosophie*, 560. In the beautiful biography by M. Yusa, *Zen & Philosophy: An Intellectual Biography of Nishida Kitarō* (Honolulu: University of Hawai'i Press, 2002), a book which is essential for understanding the intellectual trajectory of Nishida and his personal life, we read about Nishida's correspondence with Husserl, Rickert, and others via Japanese students studying in Germany, and learn that Husserl claimed that he failed to see the originality of Nishida's thought (182).

thought. Nishida, however, wanted to take up the challenge to invent a thinking that would be *more universal* than Western thought. Questioning the universality of formal logic, Nishida asks to what extent it is only a special feature of the life of history:

> Must we assume western logic to be the only logic and the eastern way of thinking simply a less-developed form of it? [...] [W]illing as I am to recognize western logic as a magnificent systematic development, and intent as I am on studying it first as one type of world logic, I wonder if even western logic is anything more than one special feature of the life of history [...]. Things like formal, abstract logic will remain the same everywhere, but concrete logic as the form of concrete knowledge cannot be independent of the specific feature of historical life.[49]

Therefore, Nishida would have to discover a new logic which is *truly* universal. On his late work Nishida came up with his famous logic of *basho*, which established the so-called 'Nishida philosophy'. The logic of *basho* is an attempt to reconcile Being, which occupies space, and Nothing, which negates space, through a philosophy of place.[50] Nishida reverses the Aristotelian logic which considers subject as substance and predicate as accident.[51] He desubstantialises the subject by putting it in a place of the predicate, or in the field of consciousness. For example, when we say a rose is red, then according to Aristotelian

---

49. Heisig, *Philosophers of Nothingness*, 36.

50. K. Nishida, 'The Logic of Basho', in *Place and Dialectic: Two Essays by Nishida Kitarō*, tr. J.W.M. Krummel and Shigenori Nagatomo (Oxford: Oxford University Press, 2012).

51. In a letter to Risaku Mutai, Nishida wrote 'This essay, "Basho," is not yet clear, but what I endeavored to do was to define consciousness logically as "that which becomes the grammatical predicate and not the grammatical subject" over against Aristotle's definition of substance as "that which becomes the grammatical subject and not the grammatical predicate".' Quoted in Yusa, *Zen & Philosophy*, 205.

logic, the rose is the subject and red is the predicate, so the predicate is a property of the rose, hence being red is subordinate to the rose as substance and grammatical subject; Nishida reverses this by *placing* the rose in the predicate red. Red is not simply a property of the rose, because now the rose is placed in red. The concept of the *basho* is that of a field of consciousness which contains. If we continue by saying that 'red is a colour', then we also place 'red' in the *basho* called 'colour', and this *basho* is also that which allows non-red to appear. Non-red is the negation of red, it negates red to nothing, so it is the nothing of 'red', but it is not that which yields redness, since both redness and non-redness are contained in another *basho*. This is also the case with actions, since each action can be identified with a causality situated in time and space. If we understand the concept of *basho* as 'that which contains', then we will find that *basho* is contained in another *basho*, and so on ad infinitum. Now, this might seem to risk giving rise to a bad 'infinity' in Hegel's sense—a problem Aristotle also encountered in seeking a first cause, and which prompted him to assign the non-moving mover as the first cause. Nishida designates absolute nothingness as the ultimate container. However, didn't Nishida therefore just replace the Prime Mover with Absolute Nothingness? And does the Absolute Nothingness itself have a place? If yes, then isn't it particular? If not, then is it not only an abstract universal? Nishida has to connect his logic of *basho* with a philosophy of history, and the absolute nothingness will have to be situated in a social-historical world.[52]

Let us restate here that it is not our aim to elaborate on the philosophies of Mou Zongsan and Kitaro Nishida, both of which deserve more dedicated monographs.[53] What we are seeking to do here is

---

52. This may sound perplexing at first glance, namely that the universal is again resituated in the local; it is perhaps consistent with one of Nishida's core concepts: oppositional unity, which was partially inspired by Nicholas of Cusa's *coincidentia oppositorum*; in *Art and Cosmotechnics*, I developed 'oppositional unity' and 'oppositional continuity' from a different source, namely Daoism.

to explain how an individuation of thinking was already practiced in the work of Mou Zongsan and Nishida. Both Mou and Nishida wanted to appropriate Western philosophy, while they were also reluctant to let go of the East; their thinking individuates in the tension between *Heimatlosigkeit* and *Heimat*. What Mou and Nishida did was not comparative philosophy; and therefore it is not entirely missing the point to criticise them for having westernised Eastern thought and to question their authenticity. But precisely, if there is a reason to oppose Eastern thinking to Western thinking, it is only so as to set up a condition of individuation, not to affirm a uniqueness or an exceptionalism. Therefore, this opposition that we find in Mou Zongsan and Nishida is not about essentialising Chinese thought or Japanese thought and making East and West strangers to one another. Instead, we might say that this opposition is only strategic, to the extent that it elucidates an incompatibility to be resolved and calls for a new structure to emerge.

There hasn't been any Mou Zongsan or Nishida in Europe yet. It is true that there is increasing interest in Chinese philosophy and Japanese philosophy under the umbrella of comparative philosophy. But where does comparison lead? Here we shouldn't forget about the work of François Jullien and other sinologists, however. Jullien often emphasised that he was *not* a comparative philosopher and that he was not interested in such a discipline, and he had good reason to say this, because his work is not about historical studies on the exchange of ideas, but rather on the gap or divergence [*écart*] between

---

53. For a more systematic comparison between the two philosophers, see Tomomi Asakura (朝倉友海), *Does East Asia Have No Philosophy? Kyoto School and New Confucianism* (「東アジアに哲学はない」のか　京都学派と新儒家) (Tokyo: Iwanami, 2014). Asakura's book is probably one of the first and so far the only systematic comparison available, which also interrogates the future of East Asian philosophy. Asakura even asks if it is possible to develop a unified theory between the two schools, a question I believe to be ill-posed, see 205–18.

two philosophies.[54] In other words, Jullien's work could be read as an effort to establish the condition of the individuation of thinking. Perhaps this view will not be easily accepted, because his approach could be reproached for positioning Chinese thought as the exotic other or the absolute other, hence condemning itself to orientalism or neo-orientalism. However, such accusations can only originate from an illusory idea of authenticity and authority.

The individuation of thinking has never become a subject in contemporary philosophical discussions. Instead, we only have comparative philosophy and postcolonialism. But aren't these themselves projects of searching for *Heimat*? The history of colonisation has to be remembered and condemned from generation to generation. If decolonisation in the non-West means negating the West, it is still a search for *Heimat*—that which is not yet contaminated or that which is able to contain the impure without being affected by it. Walter Mignolo was right when he said that the formation of nation states of the formally colonised countries wasn't decolonisation, but the continuation of colonisation.[55] And on the other hand, if the West wants to decolonise itself by imposing a political correctness upon discourse, it also risks refusing the possibility of individuation by pretending that incompatibilities don't exist. It is very probable that colonialism and imperialism will continue to exist, disguising themselves in different forms, for example the market, soft power, etc. Neither the state nor the *Großraum* will prepare for the individuation of thinking; on the contrary, they will only eliminate any such possibility, because enmity is the condition of its own survival.

Thinking doesn't individuate itself; thinking individuates through individual humans, through every one of us. It is through the individuation of thinking that we search for the universal, because the

54. F. Jullien, *L'écart et l'entre Leçon inaugurale de la Chaire sur l'altérité* (Paris: Galilée, 2012).

55. See W.D. Mignolo, *The Politics of Decolonial Investigations* (Durham, NC: Duke University Press, 2021).

universal is not something given a priori and to which everyone is subordinated. This would only be a linear and most obvious form of universality. There is a non-linear form of universality which could be understood in Kantian language as purposiveness without purpose, pleasure without interest. If we assume that there is already the universal, and go on to apply it to different things in the world, we have only recognised linear universality; but we are still far from understanding this other universality, which is not yet given. Nonetheless, it exists, and demands a new interpretation of Kant's *sensus communis*. It is the task of reason to look for the universal; and reason can only progress toward the universal through the individuation of thinking—in other words, by recognising differences, it searches for restructuralisation and diversification, and constantly does so.

We now return to the first direction concerning the relation between Asian thought and technology. Earlier we said that there is an intimate relation between these two directions, because they inform one another. We no longer live in the same epoch as Nishida and Mou Zongsan, who in their systematic writings were trying to construct a broader framework into which to absorb Western thinking (but also to go beyond it). If for Nishida and Mou Zongsan the medium of individuation is writing, today, we might need to identify other mediums if not new mediums. And that is how the question concerning technology reenters our discourse.

If the question 'What is Asia?' is valid today, it is not as an attempt to raise an ontological question, to essentialise something common to all Asian countries; nor to construct a *geistige Gestalt* in the way that Husserl or Valéry did. Such attempts will inevitably end in failure. Instead, we have been trying to show that it is difficult if not impossible to give any definite answer to such a question. Our question was rather, given such difference and asymmetricity, what could Asia contribute to contemporary thought today?

We know that today, in terms of technological development, Asian countries are moving at a much faster pace than most European countries. There is probably more modern architecture in Asian metropolitan cities than in those of Europe. Capitalism finds little resistance in the lands of Asia today, since the economy has been the priority and therefore also the most important indicator of national pride—a pride measured in GDP. Technological acceleration and economic growth have increasingly been bundled together, especially when digitalisation became a technical tendency that no country could refuse. Certain accelerationist proposals suggest that, with technological acceleration toward full automation, it is possible to dialectically negate capitalism. This imaginary is projected onto East Asia, since the East Asian countries have been highly modernised and the technological infrastructure allows faster development. However, accelerating technology does not contribute to noodiversity any more than it does to biodiversity or even technodiversity.[56] Accelerating technology will only give us a world that is becoming more and more uniform, for technology is knowledge concretised and materialised; it is the continuation of what Mizoguchi criticised, namely the West as the universal, a concept of universal which moreover is only a linear one.

It remains to be seen how Asian thought could contribute to the reconfiguration of the technological world. Maybe at least, as a first step, it can contribute to the reconfiguration of technological thought (i.e., following the corelations between biodiversity, noodiversity, and technodiversity). The two inquiries into individuation that we discussed in these two chapters are attempts to renew the discussion on 'overcoming modernity'. The attempts to undermine the 'overcoming modernity' movement by viewing it as a discourse of aesthetics, or a nationalist and culturist ideology, or as testifying to a blindness towards capitalism that appeared after the Second World

---

56. On the relation between biodiversity, noodiversity and technodiversity, see Y. Hui, 'For a Planetary Thinking', *e-flux* 114 (December 2020), <https://www.e-flux.com/journal/114/366703/for-a-planetary-thinking/>; for a more elaborated and systematic exposition of the subject, see Y. Hui, *Machine and Sovereignty* (Minneapolis: University of Minnesota Press, forthcoming 2024).

War in Japan don't really offer us a genuine occasion to philosophise. Instead, we will have to confront the Marxist critique by looking for new models of individuation in face of the new technologies that serve consumerism; we will also have to confront the temptation of essentialisation by facilitating the individuation of thinking. This search of a new theory of individuation will be a task of speculative philosophy: the search for a theory which necessarily extends and enlarges the classical theory of individuation which searched for a principle of individuation in order to explain the particularity of being. It is only with such a speculative philosophy of thinking that it will become possible to re-orient ourselves in the epoch of *Heimatlosigkeit*, and to respond to what Heidegger once said concerning the end of philosophy marked by cybernetics: 'The end of philosophy means: the beginning of the world civilization based upon Western European thinking.'

CODA

The GOOD POST-EUROPEANS

I may not be a good German, but I am a good European.

—Friedrich Nietzsche[1]

I have never in my life 'loved' some nation or collective—not the German, French, or American nation, or the working class, or whatever else there might be in this price range of loyalties. The fact is that I love only my friends and am quite incapable of any other sort of love.

—Hannah Arendt[2]

§9. AFTER NIETZSCHE, the GOOD EUROPEAN

What is Europe? What is Asia? These may no longer be good questions for us in the twenty-first century. Not only because the emergence of the imperial power of the United States has changed the course of history since the twentieth century, while the good old *Ius Publicum Europaeum* failed to address globalisation and Imperialism, as Carl Schmitt showed in his *Nomos of the Earth*, but also because the inquiry risks falling back to the 'homecoming' of past centuries by searching for an essence of a nation or a culture, which the 'great political leaders' have been promoting. A re-orientation is necessary, but that doesn't mean that we can go back to the kind of division between East and West that existed prior to the sixteenth century. If we could frankly admit that, at least in East Asia, the last few centuries have been a history of Europeanisation and subsequently Americanisation, then by admitting this and redirecting ourselves

---

1. In a letter Nietzsche wrote to his mother dated 17 August 1886 from Sils Maria; see F. Nietzsche, *Sämtliche Briefe: Kritische Studienausgabe Band 7* (Berlin: De Gruyter, 2003), 233.
2. H. Arendt and G. Scholem, *The Correspondence of Hannah Arendt and Gershom Scholem*, ed. M.L. Knott, tr. A. David (Chicago: Chicago University Press, 2017), 206.

away from this process, we all become post-Europeans. In this condition, we encounter again the problem of *Heimatlosigkeit* and the
task of thinking. The standpoint of *Heimatlosigkeit* will force us to
recognise an Other who is as *heimatlos* as ourselves.

To affirm the standpoint of *Heimatlosigkeit* is to become a true
Nietzschean. The Nietzsche of *Beyond Good and Evil*, *Genealogy of
Morality*, *Thus Spoke Zarathustra*, and *Gay Science* was a bad German.
Nationalism, for Nietzsche, was merely a replacement for the God
that had already been murdered by humans. From this point of
view, secularisation overcomes a nihilism grounded in Platonic-
Christian doctrine, but fails to fully overcome it; it still attempts
to find a replacement God. The *Vaterland* fills the vacuum of tran-
scendence left after the death of God. In other words, nationalism
is the continuation of European nihilism. Or perhaps more precisely, it could be called an 'incomplete nihilism'. After the death
of God, nationalism becomes what gives meaning to existence, as
we read in *Ecce Homo*:

> Nationalism, this *névrose nationale* with which Europe is sick,
> this perpetuation of European particularism [*Kleinstaaterei*], of
> petty politics [has] deprived Europe itself of its meaning, of its
> reason—[has] driven it into a dead-end street. —Does anyone
> besides me know the way out of this dead-end street? —A task
> that is great enough to unite nations again?[3]

A good European such as Nietzsche is someone who rejects the pathological manner of nationalist nonsense and the short-sightedness of
politicians who rise to the top with this nonsense, and who wants to
embrace Europe: 'Europe wants to be one.'[4] We now have a European
Union composed of twenty-eight countries. To some extent, we
can consider Europe as a unity, even though internal tensions and

---

3. F. Nietzsche, *Ecce Homo*, tr. W. Kaufmann and R.J. Hollingdale (New York:
    Random House, 1967), 321.

disagreement continue to exist. Europe existing as a unity is a significant historical achievement. But even after the formation of the European Union, nationalism continues to exist and may grow rapidly in view of increasing geopolitical and economic challenges—Brexit was such an example.

The world situation has changed dramatically since Nietzsche's time. But nationalism continues to grow in face of a generalised *Heimatlosigkeit* brought about by wars and planetarisation. Just as Nietzsche wanted to de-Germanise Germany, Europe might also have to de-Europeanise itself, as Stiegler claims. To de-Europeanise doesn't mean to abandon the legacy and heritage of Europe, on the contrary, it means asking how to carry the European heritage further without imposing a mechanical or linear form of universalisation. But how can we conceive of such a process? If it means an emanation from Europe to the world, as in the Enlightenment, then it may risk being a mere repetition of the past mode of unilateral movement.

That we moderns are *heimatlos* is a historical consequence. We have already abandoned the land, burned the bridge, in order to pursue the infinite, as Nietzsche describes in §124 of the *Gay Science*: in the middle of the ocean, we realise that there is nothing more fearful than the infinite, but there is no longer a home to return to because we have already broken down the bridge behind us. We are nowhere other than in the middle of the ocean, in the perplexing situation of

---

4. 'Thanks to the pathological manner in which nationalist nonsense has alienated and continues to alienate the peoples of Europe from each other; thanks as well to the short-sighted and swift-handed politicians who have risen to the top with the help of this nonsense, and have no idea of the extent to which the politics of dissolution that they practice can only be entr'acte politics, —thanks to all this and to some things that are strictly unmentionable today, the most unambiguous signs declaring that Europe wants to be one are either overlooked or wilfully and mendaciously reinterpreted.'
   F. Nietzsche, *Beyond Good and Evil: Prelude to a Philosophy of the Future*, tr. J. Norman (Cambridge: Cambridge University Press, 2002), 148 [§256].

not knowing whether it is worth advancing, while there is already no way back. Nietzsche had already described the *heimatlosige* situation for us, but we have continued to be trapped in this dilemma: choose to continue sailing into the fearful infinite, or return to a *Heimat* that no longer exists.

Heimatlosigkeit is the condition of existence in the twenty-first century. Everyone needs a home, but the home is no longer what it was, and will never again be. A home has to be thought from and against the present, and not only the past. A home thought from the present is a future home that is not yet, and will only be when the return to the past serves merely as detour and not as destination. Just as, following Patočka, Europe after the Second World War became Post-Europe, so the European will become post-European, as indeed will the non-European.

In the previous two chapters we attempted to show two distinctive ways to think about individuation as the possibility of a post-European philosophy. The first is a new model of individuation: the type of alternative to the disindividuation of the consumerist society that Stiegler tried to develop in his work. This model remains to be realised, since consumption is still the main index for measuring growth and economic development. It remains for us to develop a new critique of political economy after Marx and Stiegler. The second is to be open and to conceive an individuation of thinking that allows new thinking to emerge and diversify. However, these two cannot be separated and juxtaposed: without a critique of capitalism, we cannot advance in imagining new forms of life, and without a critique of culture, we cannot advance in facilitating diverse forms of life. It is only in this sense that we can truly talk about de-Europeanisation and the future of non-European cultures.

The post-Europeans are not orphans abandoned by history, but those who are living the logical consequences of history, namely the aftermath of planetarisation, where the consciousness and feeling of *Heimatlosigkeit* is intensified and the desire for homecoming grows. The dilemma will have to be resolved by a third path, one that is not either/or, but is also not neither/nor. In this process, one has to confront one's own natality and nationality. By refusing to be a good German, Nietzsche also resisted being a state thinker. How can one resist becoming a state thinker in the twenty-first century when statism is so deeply planted in every domain of life? Maybe at the moment when one experiences a suspension of one's nationality, and when one then becomes a modern *homo sacer*, then both the individual and all communities to which they might belong suddenly become fragile, since the state would present itself as the absolute power without which everything solid melts into air and one could experience why Nietzsche said that nationalism is a nihilism succeeding Christianity. Without undergoing such an *epochē*, it is difficult for even the best of phenomenologists to resist becoming state thinkers.... However, whenever one thinks from the standpoint of a state thinker, one falls back into a nationalism, because then the Other can only exist as either enemy or friend. Natality doesn't mean nationality, but rather an accidental thrownness onto the planet, and by which one acquires the right to be alive and to share the planet. This accidentality also means a necessary default through which one inherits certain resources given by a specific history and place; this 'original' thrownness doesn't prevent one from wandering the planet, or from accessing and adopting other resources.

The individuation of thinking can happen in any individual who carries different resources. When one is thrown into the world, one inevitably inherits the past of the family and the locality; it is also by being in the world that one is able to negotiate with this past by introducing other resources, through studying, travelling, marriage, etc. An individual is a field in which tensions and contractions are produced and resolved in order to arrive at a metastable status, namely a new thinking which discovers its own consistency. Each individual is a result of an individuation originating in the different resources which constitute its pre-individual reality. The individuation of thinking means the invention of new concepts in view of the incompatibility between two resources viewed from the present.[5] This invention could also be realised in technological terms—that is to say, firstly by creating institutions that facilitate the individuation of thinking, and secondly by intervening into the epistemological foundations of design in order to transform technologies. In this sense we can talk about 'overcoming modernity through modernity', just as Nietzsche and Nishitani attempted to 'overcome nihilism through nihilism'.[6]

§10. The Magic Tongue

In 1969, a great debate took place between the nationalist writer and representative of the Japanese romanticism Yukio Mishima and the students who participated in the social movement. Masahiko Akuta, an anarchist who later became a theatre director, challenged Mishima on his nationalism. Mishima responded 'I don't want to be anything besides a Japanese.' 'If you can speak English fluently', he continued, 'you forget that you are a Japanese. You see the reflection of a man in a shop window with a long torso and a flat nose. There is a Japanese, it is me....'[7] In reality, Mishima spoke English very well—like a Victorian aristocrat, or at least this is what we hear in the video and audio interviews he left. Mishima affirmed the inevitability of nationality owing to biological features, an attitude reinvoked some sixty-five years later by the Chinese Foreign Minister Wang Yi during a high-level meeting with two other foreign ministers of

5. One might want to recall what Gilles Deleuze and Félix Guattari said: 'We lack creation. *We lack resistance to the present.* The creation of concepts in itself calls for a future form, for a new earth and people that do not yet exist. Europeanization does not constitute a becoming but merely the history of capitalism, which prevents the becoming of subjected peoples.' *What is Philosophy?*, tr. H. Tomlinson and G. Burchell (New York: Columbia University Press, 2016).

6. To some extent, we can also attribute this to Bernard Stiegler's thinking on Heidegger and modernity.

7. *Mishima: The Last Debate* (dir. Keisuke Toyoshima, 2020), 1:18:00.

East Asia: 'No matter how yellow you dye your hair, or how sharp you make your nose, you'll never turn into a European or American, you'll never turn into a Westerner.'[8]

It is easy, and no doubt also politically effective, to reduce politics to biology and race: racism in both its politically correct and incorrect forms continues to haunt us and presents us with a vicious circle, as if there are only two options: unless one day we have the technology to produce and reproduce standardised human beings like those white people dreamt of by Kang Youwei, then we can avoid this fatalism—this might well be a transhumanist agenda of peace. However, this universalism is already in itself a racism since only one race is affirmed and the rest has to assimilate, i.e. by becoming white. But if this is not the future we desire, then we will have to look elsewhere for a solution. Technology, as prosthesis, might allow us equal rights to access resources, and allow everyone to actualise their potential without being hindered by geographical factors. However, current industrial technology, and the personalised consumerism it promises, is moving against such possibilities.

We might want to return here to another technical organ, the tongue. The tongue and the hands were the primordial technical organs, although we tend to remember the relation between the invention of tools and liberation of the hands and forget the relation between the invention of language and the development of the tongue. The tongue determines both taste and the ability to speak. On the one hand, the tongue is central to the *Heimat* since it is that which makes taste possible, and therefore enables a physio-psychological connection between body and the *Heimat*. Recall how, after the first taste of a bowl of *shirogohan* in Germany, Nishitani was able to reconnect with Japan through his taste buds.

---

8. 'China Dismisses Criticism of Top Diplomat's Comments Appearing to Push for Race-based Alliance', *AP News*, 5 July 2023, <https://apnews.com/article/china-japan-korea-race-controversy-b1fb99824d31b3f88a0893cacf6f54f0>.

It is the tongue that is able to know the *aji* (taste) of food, not the stomach or the intestines. A wise man [*sapiens*] is a taster, as we are told by Isidore de Sevilla:

> The word 'sapiens' [wise man] is derived from 'sapor' [taste] (*Sapiens dictus a sapore*) for just as the sense of taste is able to discern the flavours [*sapore*] of different foods, so too is the wise man able to discern objects and their causes since he recognizes each one as distinct and is able to judge them with an instinct for truth.[9]

The taste of the tongue and taste for objects are not without connection. Taste is not only about sensual pleasure, but also implies a sensibility and an intuitive understanding which we may call judgement.[10]

It is the tongue that makes speaking and language possible. The fact that Latin reserves the word tongue [*lingua*] for language [*lingua*] is not without profundity. The original tongue is the mother tongue—the one that is considered to be the most spontaneous and embodied language. The mother tongue is the correlate of the fatherland. The fatherland and mother tongue would be purely abstract without the tongue. It was no coincidence that in the eighteenth century, Herder and the Romantics tried to give a philosophical sense to both fatherland and mother tongue. For example, in his lecture 'On the Different Methods of Translating', Schleiermacher emphasised the uniqueness of the mother tongue: it is organic, while translation is mechanical. The second or third language that one masters

---

9. Cited in G. Agamben, *Taste*, tr. C. Francis (London: Seagull Books, 2017), 4.

10. See Campanella, *Theologia*, book 16, 'It is not by deliberation that man judges whether a spirit is a devil or an angel [...]. It is rather by sensitivity and an intuitive understanding that he is persuaded [...] just as we immediately recognize the taste of bread and wine with our tongue.' Cited in Agamben, *Taste*, 23–24.

is never as organic as the mother tongue, since the communication of information becomes more important, and tones and intonation are set aside. This distinction could be applied today to machine translation and mother tongues: in a way, Schleiermacher anticipated a criticism that is now directed against AI machine translation. By the same token, one could argue that it is pointless to learn any foreign language since the machine could do a much better job in seconds, and hence free human beings from years of learning and practicing. It is also for this reason that originality can only come out of the mother tongue:

> For whoever acknowledges the creative power of language, as it is one with the character of the nation [*Eigenthümlichkeit des Volkes*], must also concede that [...] no one adheres to his language only mechanically, as if it were something externally attached to him like a strap and as if one could as easily harness another language for one's thought as one would exchange a team of horses [*Gespann*]; rather, every writer can produce original work only in his mother tongue [*Muttersprache*], and therefore the question cannot even be raised how he would have written his works in another language.[11]

It was probably ignorance on Schleimacher's part that he didn't realise that there are many people on this earth who cannot write in their mother tongue, since there is no corresponding writing system for their language. These are the mother tongues which are undermined as dialects and whose writing systems are suppressed in favour of the unity of a nation. Unlike Derrida, who called himself a

---

11. F. Schleiermacher, 'From "On the Different Methods of Translating"', in *Theories of Translation: An Anthology of Essays from Dryden to Derrida*, eds. R. Schulte and J. Biguenet (Chicago: University of Chicago Press, 1992), 50; also cited by Y. Yildiz, *Beyond the Mother Tongue: The Postmonolingual Condition* (New York: Fordham University Press, 2012), 8–9, translation modified.

Franco-Maghrebian—someone born in North Africa in a Jewish family but who was exposed to the French language as a first language—the first language of such people can't become written language, so the language they write in is probably already their second or third language. The opposition between mechanism and organism that was central to Schleiermacher's argument had been the foundation of modern European philosophy since the eighteenth century, and one might suspect that the distinction between mother tongue and second or third language in Schleiermacher was derived from the implications of this epistemological understanding. The term 'organic' was a counterconcept to that of mechanism and consequently it stood for what philosophy, community, nation, and state ought to be. Kant's *Critique of Judgment*, as I argued in *Recursivity and Contingency*, imposed an organic condition of philosophising, which was then adopted by the idealists.[12] Organism is associated with community, nation, feeling and mother tongue. At the beginning of the twentieth century, Eastern thinkers identified Eastern thought with organism and the West with mechanism—a line of thought we can find in the historical work of Joseph Needham as well as in the thought of the Kyoto philosopher Kiyoshi Miki, who proposed a return to the original 'organic' Japanese culture as a way to overcome Western modernity.[13] However, I have also argued that cybernetics has put an end to this organic condition of philosophising, since, as Norbert Wiener claimed and as we are witnessing today, the theoretical opposition between machine and organism seems to have already been surpassed by cybernetic machines. In other words, the distinction between mechanism and organism is

12. We have elaborated on this theme in the trilogy *Recursivity and Contingency* (2019), *Art and Cosmotechnics* (2021) and *Machine and Sovereignty* (forthcoming, 2024).

13. K. Miki, 'Philosophy of Technology', *MKZ* 7 (三木清全集・第七巻) (Tokyo: Iwanami Shoten, 1985), 324–25; for a more detailed discussion, see Hui, *Art and Cosmotechnics*, 267–69.

no longer a good criterion by which to understand languages: we cannot say that ChatGPT is merely mechanical in the same way that a clock might have been described as mechanical in the eighteenth century, for instance. If in the eighteenth century this opposition had its epistemological importance, today insisting upon such an opposition risks being merely ideological.

The tongue changes the past, not only as that which associates taste and past experience, but also by learning to speak in a different language. In learning a new language one's relation to one's past is also altered, especially for those who are in exile, as was the case for Hannah Arendt, Milan Kundera, and others. One is forced to train the muscle of the tongue to move in a new way, until eventually it finds the previous muscular movements unfamiliar. Arendt recalled in her 1943 essay 'We, Refugees' that the acquisition of the English language had an almost magical effect: by the second year of immigration, one even could hardly remember one's mother tongue:

> It is true we sometimes raise objections when we are told to forget about our former work; and our former ideals are usually hard to throw over if our social standard is at stake. With the language, however, we find no difficulties: after a single year optimists are convinced they speak English as well as their mother tongue; and after two years they swear solemnly that they speak English better than any other language—their German is a language they hardly remember.[14]

Twenty years later, during a 1964 TV interview conducted by Günther Gaus with the title '*Was bleibt*? [What Remains?]', we hear Arendt confessing 'I was telling myself: What is to be done? It is not really the German language, after all, that has gone mad. And in the second place, nothing can replace the mother tongue.'[15]

14. H. Arendt, 'We Refugees', <https://www.documenta14.de/de/south/35_we_refugees>.

Arendt admitted that there are people who could forget their mother tongue, while she always spoke with a strong accent and often happened not to express herself in an idiomatic fashion.[16] When she talked about the importance of having a large archive of German poems, Arendt couldn't remember the idiom '*im Hinterkopf*' and switched to the English 'in the back of the mind'.[17] It is difficult to determine whether it is the mother tongue or the foreign language that is in the back of the mind.

It would be a mistake to think that in the future, with the advancement of machine learning, one will not have to learn any foreign languages because AI can do translation for humans effortlessly. It is true that today one can effectively use a digital apparatus to communicate with foreigners—a huge opportunity for tourism: Stiegler told me the story of how, in 2018, he was refused entry by several hotels in Shanghai until he came upon one where the reception staff took out a translation device to communicate with him. However, if one reduces language to a medium of communication, one undermines the tongue and its relation to thinking. In *The Two Sources of Morality and Religion* (1932), Henri Bergson made a remark on learning a foreign language which deserves mention here. Commenting on the patriotism of a Frenchman who is a professor of German and that of an ordinary Frenchman, he argued that they are not the same. A professor of German, although he is ready to die for France during the war like any other patriotic Frenchmen, is not able to have the same hate toward Germany as others:

> A professor of German was just as patriotic as any other Frenchman, just as ready to lay down his life, just as 'worked up' even against Germany; yet it was not the same thing. One

---

15. Cited in J. Derrida, *Monolingualism of the Other or, The Prosthesis of Origin*, tr. P. Mensah (Stanford, CA: Stanford University Press, 1998), 85n.
16. Cited in Derrida, *Monolingualism of the Other*, 90n.
17. See Yildiz, *Beyond the Mother Tongue*, 220.

corner was set apart. Anyone who is thoroughly familiar with the language and literature of a people cannot be wholly its enemy.[18]

We could probably understand Arendt's complicit relation to the German language and to Germany in terms of what Bergson says here. The case is obvious in Arendt, a Jewish woman in exile whose mother tongue was German. As Bergson indicates, this complicit relation also exists between the countries and those who master their languages. It was difficult for a Chinese connoisseur of Japanese culture and language such as Lu Xun to treat Japan in the same way as other Chinese during war time; and it is probably inappropriate to place Mishima, Takeuchi, and Nishitani in an abstract category of nationalism along with other Japanese. They all carried resources they acquired from elsewhere, however, whether that could allow an individuation to take place is another question. The conclusion that Bergson drew from his wartime experience was that the 'mastery of a foreign tongue, by making possible the impregnation of the mind by the corresponding literature and civilization, may at one stroke do away with the prejudice ordained by nature against foreigners in general'.[19] We must, however, interpret what Bergson says here by understanding language as an access to a particular resource, which is also a constituent of the pre-individual reality; without access to this resource via language, one misses the chance of individuation, and in the end an immigrant would reduce himself or herself to mere labour force available for exportation.

It is astonishing when we see the tongue determining both *Heimat* and *Heimatlosigkeit*, in an entirely non-abstract way. The tongue is where the contradiction meets, the contradiction between nostalgia for *Heimat* and the desire to not be at home. The tongue, along with its taste buds, determines the belonging of the body to the

18. H. Bergson, *The Two Sources of Morality and Religion*, tr. R.A. Audra and C. Brereton (Westport, CT: Greenwood, 1974), 275.

19. Ibid., 275.

fatherland—no matter how good the Japanese restaurants in Germany are, they may never completely satisfy the taste buds of a Japanese; while the tongue with the flexibility of its muscle allows one to overcome the limits that the taste buds have set and to go beyond the mother tongue. The profoundness of language beyond communication, which Herder and Schleiermacher called organicity, if it really exists, doesn't lie in the contemplation of the grammatical structure of the language, but rather in its everyday use and practice. For in the end, it is not the mind alone that is functioning in the process of speaking. To learn a new language is to perform gymnastics of the tongue and the lips until an automatism is gained. It is even more difficult for someone who has lost half of their tongue to learn new languages, because it involves retraining the whole motor-sensory system and struggling with the coordination of muscles—in this case the tongue itself also becomes prosthetic. However, one can nonetheless achieve it by shadowing, reading aloud, reciting, listening to recordings of one's own voice, etc. In the end, both the organicity that Schleiermacher aspires to and the mechanicity of language learning are ways of acquiring automatism. One might want to recall Denis Diderot's *The Paradox of Acting*, where we read that a great comedian can only become a fine player by repetitively practicing to the point of becoming an *automaton*.[20] Not only does the difference between what is original and what is acquired become arbitrary, but also the original demands the artificial.

* * *

20. See D. Diderot, *The Paradox of Acting*, tr. W.H. Pollock (London: Chatto & Windus, 1883), 30–31. In a note, Diderot cites François-René Molé, who talked about his experience of acting: 'I was not pleased with myself. I let myself go too much; I felt the situation too deeply; I became the personage instead of the actor playing it; I lost my self-control. I was true to Nature as I might be in private; the perspective of the stage demands something different. The piece is to be played again in a few days first appeared like *automata*; afterwards they became fine players' (italics mine).

Looking back from the third decade of the century, the longing for *Heimat* reemerged in view of the failure of the first wave of globalisation and the last struggle of the neoliberal order. On the front of geopolitics, we find increasing resistance against American imperialism along with the homogenisation that it brought about. Such resistance in the name of national security ends up in calls for autonomy and state sovereignty on one hand, and a multipolar world on the other. But how different are they from the call for *Heimat*, for the return to the state in the name of the people? That is however not a solution that we should look to in order to resolve the planetary crisis in the twenty-first century, since increasing competition between states will never put an end to wars and to the intensifying exploitation of the planet. The longing for *Heimat* has become a global melodrama in the past century, expressing itself as antagonism between self and other, leading to conflicts of all kinds. Therefore, we must envision our journey by looking at it from the standpoint of *Heimatlosigkeit*. If Heidegger was able to claim that 'homelessness is the destiny of the world', then this destiny can only be overcome, not by returning to the *Heimat*, but by seeking a new definition of locality and diversity. A locality in which one can discover new models and new configurations of individuation that could resist the tendency of disindividuation intrinsic to the *homo consumericus* and *homo economicus* who values economic freedom over everything else and reduces freedom to arbitrariness, as well as the latest nihilist, *homo deus*, who wants to elevate a human individual over all kinds of non-humans to the status of a prosthetic God, and who wants to leave the earth to be 'among the stars'. In response to Derrida's claim that philosophy is intrinsically European and Heidegger's proposal for a future of thinking (of Being), then, a post-European philosophy has to be one that is able to go beyond the ideological opposition between East and West, the stereotypical opposition between collectivism and individualism, and the philosophical opposition between Being and Nothing; and in which such going beyond is not a neutralisation of differences, but an individuation of thinking.

BIBLIOGRAPHY

Agamben, Giorgio. *Taste*, tr. C. Francis. London: Seagull Books, 2017.

Arendt, Hannah. *The Human Condition*. Chicago: Chicago University Press, 2002.
——. 'We Refugees', *Documenta14*, <https://www.documenta14.de/de/south/35_we_refugees>.
——, and Gershom Scholem. *The Correspondence of Hannah Arendt and Gershom Scholem*, ed. M. L. Knott, tr. A. David. Chicago: Chicago University Press, 2017.

Asakura, Tomomi (朝倉友海). *Does East Asia Have No Philosophy? Kyoto School and New Confucianism* (「東アジアに哲学はない」のか　京都派と新儒家). Tokyo: Iwanami, 2014.

Bergson, Henri. *Two Sources of Morality and Religion*, tr. R.A. Audra and C. Brereton. Westport: Greenwood, 1974.

Borradori, Giovanna. *Philosophy in a Time of Terror: Dialogues with Jurgen Habermas and Jacques Derrida*. Chicago: University of Chicago Press, 2004.

Brown, Chris. *Sovereignty, Rights and Justice*. Cambridge: Polity, 2002.

Chen, K.H. *Asia as Method: Toward Deimperialization*. Durham: Duke University Press, 2010.

Crépon, Marc. *Altérités de l'Europe*. Paris: Galilée, 2006.
——. 'Fear, Courage, Anger: The Socratic Lesson', in I. Chvatík and E. Abrams (eds.), *Jan Patočka and the Heritage of Phenomenology*. Dordrecht: Springer, 2011.

Dastur, Françoise. 'L'Europe et ses philosophes: Nietzsche, Husserl, Heidegger, Patocka', *Revue Philosophique de Louvain* 104: 1 (2006): 1–22.

Deleuze, Gilles and Félix Guattari. *What is Philosophy?*, tr. H. Tomlinson and G. Burchell. New York: Columbia University Press, 1996.

Diderot, Denis. *The Paradox of Acting*, tr. W. H. Pollock. London: Chatto & Windus, 1883.

Derrida, Jacques. *L'autre Cap*. Paris: Minuit, 1991.
——. *The Other Heading Reflections on Today's Europe*, tr. P.-A. Brault and M.B. Naas. Indianapolis: Indiana University Press, 1992.
——. *Monolingualism of the Other or, The Prosthesis of Origin*, tr. P. Mensah. Stanford, CA: Stanford University Press, 1998.

Ellul, Jacques. *The Technological Society*. New York: Vintage, 1964.

Glissant, Édouard. *Poetics of Relation*, tr. B. Wing. Ann Arbor: University of Michigan Press, 1997.
——. 'Creolization in the Making of the Americas', *Caribbean Quarterly* 54, 1–2 (2008): 81–89.

Gu Yanwu. *Ri Zhi Lu* (《日知錄》), chapter 13, <https://ctext.org/wiki. pl?if=gb&chapter=614214>.

Günther, Gotthard. 'Heidegger und die Weltgeschichte des Nichts', in U. Guzzoni (ed.), *Nachdenken über Heidegger: eine Bestandsaufnahme*. Hildesheim: Gerstenberg, 1980.

Habermas, Jürgen and Jacques Derrida. 'February 15, or What Binds Europeans Together: A Plea for a Common Foreign Policy, Beginning in the Core of Europe', in Lasse Thomassen (ed.), *The Derrida-Habermas Reader*, 270–77. Edinburgh: Edinburgh University Press, 2006.

Hegel, G.W.F. *Philosophy of History*, tr. J. Sibree. New York: Dover, 1956.

Heidegger, Martin. *An Introduction to Metaphysics*, tr. R. Mannheim. Garden City, NJ: Anchor, 1961.
——. *Poetry, Language, Thought*. New York: Harper and Row, 1971.
——. *What is Called Thinking?*, tr. F.D. Wieck and J. Glenn Gray. New York: Harper & Row, 1968.
——. 'Language in the Poem A Discussion on George Trakl's Poetic Art', in P.D. Hertz (tr.), *On the Way to Language*. New York: Harper & Row, 1971.
——. *On Time and Being*, tr. J. Stambaugh. New York: Harper & Row, 1972.
——. 'The Pathway', in T.F. O'Meara (tr.), *Listening Journal of Religion and Culture* 8: 1–3 (1973): 37.
——. 'The Age of the World Picture', in W. Lovitt (tr.), *The Question Concerning Technology and Other Essays*. New York: Harper & Row, 1977.
——. *Hölderlins Hymne »Der Ister« GA 53*. Frankfurt am Main: Vittorio Klostermann, 1993.
——. 'Letter on Humanism', in W. McNeill (ed.), *Pathmarks*, tr. F.A. Capuzzi. Cambridge: Cambridge University Press, 1998.

Heisig, James. *Philosophers of Nothingness: An Essay on the Kyoto School*. Honolulu: University of Hawai'i Press, 2001.

Hiromatsu, Wataru. *On 'Overcoming Modernity': A Perspective on the History of Shōwa Thought* (〈近代の超克〉論—昭和思想史への一視角). Tokyo: Kōdansha, 1989.

Hui, Yuk. *The Question Concerning Technology in China: An Essay in Cosmotechnics*. Falmouth: Urbanomic, 2016.

——. *Recursivity and Contingency*. London: Rowman and Littlefield International, 2019.

——. *Art and Cosmotechnics*. New York and Minneapolis: e-flux/University of Minnesota Press, 2021.

——. *Machine and Sovereignty*. Minneapolis: University of Minnesota Press, forthcoming 2024.

Husserl, Edmund. 'Philosophy and the Crisis of European Man'. Lecture delivered in Vienna, 10 May 1935, <https://www.hs-augsburg.de/~harsch/germanica/Chronologie/20Jh/Husserl/hus_kris.html>.

——. *The Crisis of European Sciences and Transcendental Phenomenology: An Introduction to Phenomenological Philosophy*, tr. D. Carr. Evanston, IL: Northwestern University Press, 1970.

——. 'Foundational Investigations of the Phenomenological Origin of the Spatiality of Nature: The Originary Ark, the Earth, Does Not Move', in M. Merleau-Ponty, *Husserl at the Limits of Phenomenology Including Texts by Edmund Husserl*, tr. L. Lawlor and B. Bergo, 117–31. Evanston: Northwestern University Press, 2001.

Jullien, François. *L'écart et l'entre Leçon inaugurale de la Chaire sur l'altérité*. Paris: Galilée, 2012.

——. 'Between Is Not Being', *Theory, Culture & Society* 40:4–5 (2023): 239–49.

Kang Youwei (康有為). *The Book of Great Harmony* (《大同書》), <https://ctext.org/wiki.pl?if=gb&res=306261>.

Kissinger, Henry. 'How the Enlightenment Ends', *The Atlantic*, June 2018.

Kleingeld, Pauline. 'Romantic Cosmopolitanism: Novalis's "Christianity or Europe"', *Journal of the History of Philosophy* 46:2 (2008): 269–84.

Kosaka, Masaaki et al. *The Standpoint of World History and Japan* (世界史的場と日本). Tokyo: Chūōkōron-sha, 1943.

Löwith, Karl. *Weltgeschichte und Heilsgeschehen: Zur Kritik der Geschichtsphilosophie*. Stuttgart: J.B. Metzlersche, 1983.

Lyotard, Jean-François. *The Inhuman: Reflections on Time*, tr. G. Bennington and R. Bowlby. Stanford, CA: Stanford University Press, 1991.

Maruyama, Masao (丸山眞男). 'The Kosō of Historical Consciousness' (「歴史意識の『古層』」), in *Collected Work of Masao Maruyama Vol. 10* (『丸山眞男集第10巻』). Tokyo: Iwanami, 1996.

Matsui, Nobuyuki. '"Overcoming Modernity," Capital, and Life System: Divergence of "Nothing" in the 1970s and 1980s', *The Journal of East Asian Philosophy* (2023), <https://doi.org/10.1007/s43493-023-00020-9>.

Mignolo, Walter D. *The Politics of Decolonial Investigations*. Durham, NC: Duke University Press, 2021.

Miki, Kiyoshi. 'Philosophy of Technology', in *MKZ* 7 (三木清全集・第 七巻). Tokyo: Iwanami Shoten, 1985.

Mizoguchi, Yuzo (溝口雄三). *China as Method*, tr. L. Youchong (林右崇). Taipei: National Institute for Compilation and Translation, 1999.

Nietzsche, Friedrich. *Ecce Homo*, tr. W. Kaufmann and R.J. Hollingdale. New York: Random House, 1967.
——. *The Will to Power*, tr. W. Kaufmann and R.J. Hollingdale. New York: Vintage, 1968.
——. *Beyond Good and Evil Prelude to a Philosophy of the Future*, tr. J. Norman. Cambridge: Cambridge University Press, 2002.
——. *Sämtliche Briefe: Kritische Studienausgabe Band 7*. Berlin: De Gruyter, 2003.

Nishida, Kitaro. 'The Logic of Basho', in J.W.M. Krummel and S. Nagatomo (tr.), *Place and Dialectic Two Essays by Nishida Kitarō*. Oxford: Oxford University Press, 2012.

Nishitani, Keiji, et al. *The Standpoint of World History and Japan* (『世界史的立場 と日本』). Tokyo: Chūō Kōron, 1943.
——. 'The Experience of Eating Rice' (飯を喰つた經驗), in *NKC* 20 (西谷啓治著作集). Tokyo: Shobunsha, 1990, 196–202.
——. *The Self-Overcoming of Nihilism*, tr. G. Parkes with S. Aihara. New York: SUNY Press, 1990.
——. *On Buddhism*, tr. S. Yamamoto and R.E. Carter. New York: SUNY Press, 2006.

Novalis. *Notes for a Romantic Encyclopedia: Das Allgemeine Brouillon*, ed., tr. D.W. Wood. New York: SUNY Press, 2007.

Novotný, Karel. 'Europe, Post-Europe, and Eurocentrism', in F. Tava and D.Meacham (eds.), *Thinking After Europe Jan Patočka and Politics*. London: Rowman and Littlefield International, 2016.

Patočka, Jan. 'Europa und Nach-Europa. Die nacheuropäische Epoche und ihre geistigen Probleme', in K. Nellen and J. Němec (eds.), *Ketzerische Essays zur Philosophie der Geschichte und ergänzende Schriften*. Stuttgart: Klett-Cotta, 1988.
——. 'The Obligation to Resist Injustice', in E. Kohák (ed.), *Philosophy and Selected Writings*. Chicago: Chicago University Press, 1989.
——. *Liberté et sacrifice Ecrits politiques*. Grenoble: Jérôme Millon, 1993.
——. *Heretical Essays In the Philosophy of History*, tr. E. Kobak. Chicago: Open Court, 1996.
——. *Plato and Europe*, tr. P. Lom. Stanford, CA: Stanford University Press, 2002.
——. *Europa und Nach-Europa: Zur Phänomenologie einer Idee*. Baden-Baden: Karl Alber, 2020.
——. 'On the Soul in Plato (1972)', in E. Plunkett and I. Chvatík (eds.), *The Selected Writings of Jan Patočka: Care for the Soul*, tr. A. Zucker. London: Bloomsbury, 2022.

Pelluchon, Corine. *Les Lumières à l'âge du vivant*. Paris: Seuil, 2022.

Young, Julian. 'Heidegger's Heimat', *International Journal of Philosophical Studies* 19:2 (2011): 285–93.

Rilke, Rainer Maria. *Briefe in Zwei Bänden Band 2*. Wiesbaden: Insel Verlag, 1950.

Schleiermacher, Friedrich. 'From "On the Different Methods of Translating"', in R. Schulte and J. Biguenet (eds.), *Theories of Translation: An Anthology of Essays from Dryden to Derrida*, 36–54. Chicago: University of Chicago Press, 1992.

Schmitt, Carl. 'Die Einheit der Welt', in *Staat, Großraum, Nomos Arbeiten aus den Jahren 1916–1969*. Berlin: Duncker und Humblot, 1995.

Schuback, Marcia Sá Cavalcante. 'Sacrifice and Salvation: Jan Patočka's Reading of Heidegger on the Question of Technology', in *Jan Patočka and the Heritage of Phenomenology*, 23–37. Dordrecht: Springer, 2010.

Simondon, Gilbert. *Individuation in Light of Notions of Form and Information*, tr. T. Adkins. Minneapolis: University of Minnesota Press, 2020.

Sloterdijk, Peter. *Infinite Mobilization Towards a Critique of Political Kinetics*, tr. S. Berjan. Cambridge: Polity, 2020.
——, and Sven Michaelsen. 'Man denkt an mich, also bin ich' (2014), <https://sz-magazin.sueddeutsche.de/wissen/man-denkt-an-mich-also-bin-ich-80778>.

Spengler, Oswald. *Man and Technics: A Contribution to a Philosophy of Life*, tr. C.F. Atkinson. London: Allen & Unwin, 1932.

Stiegler, Bernard. 'Oedipus, Epimetheus', tr. R. Beardsworth, *Technema* 3 (1996): 69–.

——. *Technics and Time 1. The Fault of Epimetheus.* Stanford, CA: Stanford University Press, 1998.

——. *Constituer l'Europe 1. Dans un monde sans vergogne.* Paris: Galilée, 2005.

——. *Technics and Time 2: Disorientation*, tr. S. Barker. Stanford, CA: Stanford University Press, 2008.

——. 'The Magic Skin; or, The Franco-European Accident of Philosophy after Jacques Derrida.' *Qui Parle: Critical Humanities and Social Sciences* 18:1 (2009): 97–110.

Takeuchi, Yoshimi. *Overcoming Modernity* (近代の超克). Tokyo: Chikuma Shobō, 1983.

——. *What is Modernity?*, tr. R. Calichman. New York: Columbia University Press, 2005.

Toynbee, Arnold. *The World and the West.* Oxford University Press, 1953.

Valéry, Paul. 'The Crisis of the Mind', in J.R. Lawler (ed.), *Valéry: An Anthology.* London and Henley: Routledge and Kegan Paul, 1977.

Watsuji, Tetsurō. *Climate and Culture: A Philosophical Study*, tr. G. Bownas. Westport, CT: Greenwood Press, 1961.

Wang, Yuanhua (王元化). 'Talks about Philosophy and Culture of China and the West' (关于中西哲学与文化的对话), *Journal of Literature, History and Philosophy* (《文史哲》) 2 (2002): 5–8.

Williams, David. *The Philosophy of Japanese Wartime Resistance: A Reading, with Commentary, of the Complete Texts of the Kyoto School Discussions of 'The Standpoint of World History and Japan'.* London: Routledge, 2014.

Yildiz, Yasemin. *Beyond the Mother Tongue: The Postmonolingual Condition.* New York: Fordham University Press, 2012.

Yusa, Michiko. *Zen & Philosophy An Intellectual Biography of Nishida Kitarō.* Honolulu: University of Hawai'i Press, 2002.

INDEX OF NAMES

INDEX OF SUBJECTS

Published in 2024 by

Urbanomic Media Ltd
The Old Lemonade Factory
Windsor Quarry
Falmouth TR11 3EX
United Kingdom
www.urbanomic.com

Sequence Press
88 Eldridge Street
New York, NY 10002
United States
www.sequencepress.com

© Sequence Press, 2024
All rights reserved. No part of this publication may be reproduced in any
form by any electronic or mechanical means without permission in writing
from the publisher.

Design: General Working Group

Set in Baskerville 10 Pro and Berthold Akzidenz Grotesk

Cover image: Detail from *Lithosphere (section 1)*, 2023, by
Florian Pumhösl. Oil on Finnpappe, mounted on wood, 30 ⅛ × 36 ⅛
inches (76.5 × 91.8 cm). Photo by Stephen Faught. Courtesy the artist and
Miguel Abreu Gallery.

A special note of thanks to Flint Jamison.

ISBN: 979-8-9854235-1-8

US Library of Congress Control Number: 2024932647

A full catalogue record of this book is available from the British Library.

Printed and bound in the UK by Short Run Press

Distributed by the MIT Press
Cambridge, Massachusetts and London, England

Yuk Hui is currently Professor of Philosophy at Erasmus University Rotterdam. He wrote his doctoral thesis under Bernard Stiegler (1952–2020) at Goldsmiths College in London, and obtained his habilitation in philosophy from Leuphana University in Germany. He has been professor at the City University of Hong Kong and visiting professor at the University of Tokyo and the China Academy of Art. Hui is the author of several titles including *On the Existence of Digital Objects* (University of Minnesota Press, 2016), *The Question Concerning Technology in China: An Essay in Cosmotechnics* (Urbanomic, 2016), *Recursivity and Contingency* (Rowman & Littlefield, 2019), *Art and Cosmotechnics* (e-flux/University of Minnesota Press, 2021) and *Machine and Sovereignty: For a Planetary Thinking* (University of Minnesota Press, 2024).